THE LEGO NINJAGO MOVIE

THE MAKING OF THE MOVIE

WRITTEN BY TRACEY MILLER-ZARNEKE

CONTENTS

Down on the water • Final render • Ninjago City is a lush and vibrant location – and ripe for invasion by four-armed villains!

THE MAKING OF THE MOVIE

VEHICLES 158

FOREWORD

THE LEGO® NINJAGO™ MOVIE is one of my favourite ever projects to have been a part of. The character of Lloyd Garmadon, despite being a LEGO cartoon, is one of the most complex roles I've ever tackled.

He's labelled an outsider because of the simple fact that his father is considered "the worst guy on earth". As much as he wants to disassociate himself with his evil lineage, he's still desperately trying to understand who his father is – partially because he's scared that he may have inherited some of his unflattering traits, and partially because he still believes his father might actually be a good person underneath his evil exterior.

As an actor, there's a lot for me to sink my teeth into, and I have to admit, I found myself performing the final scenes of the movie with tears streaming down my face. As you can imagine, it was weird for everyone in the recording booth to see me getting so emotional about the family dynamics of plastic yellow figurines.

All of this is a testament to the filmmakers and creative forces behind the project who have spent years obsessing over ever tiny detail – the stunning visuals, nuanced storyline, relatable characters and humour that plays equally well to my friends who are in their 30s as it does to my nephews who are all under the age of 5.

The imagination of the creative team leaves me in awe, and I just feel fortunate to be along for the ride. I'd be a happy man if all I did was new installations of THE LEGO NINJAGO MOVIE for the rest of my career.

DAVE FRANCO
– Lloyd, the Green Ninja

TIMELINE

Bringing the six ninja of Ninjago City to the big screen was no secret mission – in fact, the making of THE LEGO® NINJAGO® MOVIE™ required the teamwork of hundreds of talented artists, technology wizards and film-makers across three countries. Key moments in their international cinematic adventure are mapped out here.

Small screen, big image · The LEGO NINJAGO television series is now in its seventh season and has also included a TV Special entitled "The Day of the Departed".

1. FROM SMALL SCREEN TO BIG SCREEN

For six years prior to its theatrical debut in 2017, the action of Ninjago City lit up small screens as a top-rated show on the Cartoon Network. Ninjago City has also existed in the real world for just as long via LEGO sets that take up residence in the playrooms and imaginations of fans around the globe.
"Our vision for the characters, their designs and personalities all started with the source material, but we knew we didn't want to just copy what was in the show. We wanted to evolve the designs for the big screen, giving the audience something new and fresh", explains Director Charlie Bean.

2. A GLOBAL TEAM

A trio of creative forces came together to craft the movie: Warner Bros. Studios in California, Animal Logic in Australia and the LEGO Group in Denmark all contributed in a big way to the making of the film. The main concepts, story and script were generated between Warner Bros. and Animal Logic; Animal Logic was home base for the film production process and the LEGO Group came up with ideas for character, vehicle and set builds for both movie-making and toy-producing efforts. "Together we've created the LEGO version of a martial arts movie and a kaiju movie all in one", explains Producer Dan Lin. "Many films in those genres have an almost operatic quality to them – big emotions, over the top characters and super dynamic action. The idea of telling a story that way was really intriguing and made me want to see our cast of characters play on that stage", adds Writer/Director Paul Fisher. "A LEGO minifigure on the big screen has very different design requirements to a minifigure for real-world manufacture, but with plenty of cooperative work between Animal Logic and the fantastic design team at the LEGO Group, we were able to push the characters to be as memorable, unique and engaging as possible", notes Production Designer Kim Taylor.

Crazy for characters • LEGO designers in Billund, Denmark – such as Paul Marion Wood, Niels Milan Pedersen, Jakob Rune Nielsen, Stewart Whitehead and Esa Petteri Nousiainen (above, left to right) – conceived the character line-up for THE LEGO NINJAGO MOVIE.

Colours and characters and contraptions • *Photo, Madeleine Purdy* • The team at Animal Logic in Sydney constantly referred to the LEGO palette and brick library in their production design, art direction and modelling choices.

Words to live with and animate by • The script plots out the movie with words and inspires the visuals that illustrate and, in turn, often inspire more words.

3. SCRIPTING THE STORY

The scripting and storyboarding processes work in tandem, with words inspiring pictures and pictures inspiring words along the same cinematic path. However, navigating onto that path in the first place is the greatest creative challenge. "We tried a LOT of different versions of the story, including a time-travel movie with a giant mechanical mongoose fighting a very big snake. I think we ultimately landed on the right story for the first movie, but the process proved that there are definitely more Ninjago stories to be told", recalls Director Charlie Bean. Paul Fisher and Bob Logan were initially brought in as scriptwriters for the project, but in time their roles expanded to that of directors along with Bean. Meanwhile, Head of Story Maggie Kang and her crew drew thousands of story panels to portray the movie in a shot-by-shot, comic-book manner of visual scripting, sorting out timing, expressions and initial camera suggestions as part of their scope of work. LEGO Senior Creative Director Simon Lucas adds that "we always knew that we wanted to tell a story about Lloyd, the Green Ninja, who just wants a good relationship with his dad – but unfortunately, his dad is Lord Garmadon – who just wants to invade and conquer the city!"

4. ANIMATIC CREATION

Story panels are passed along to the editing team that adds temporary dialogue, sound effects and music to form a story reel, also known as an animatic. This is essentially a rough cut of the film, and the first chance to see how the sequences will play out on a big screen. Like viewing a moving comic book, the animatic allows the creative teams to explore and refine ideas and scenes. Throughout the production process of the movie, each shot is updated until the initial rough cut eventually transforms into a fully animated, full-colour movie.

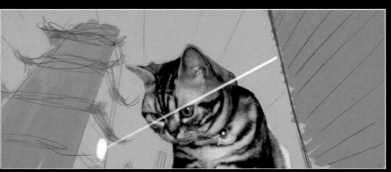

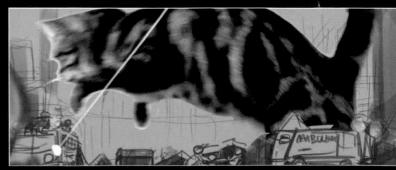

Cat-astrophe • *Storyboard art, Paul Fisher and Eric Ramsey* • Live-action cat film is combined with story panels to plot out the destruction of Ninjago City buildings.

"With THE LEGO NINJAGO MOVIE it feels like we're taking LEGO movies to the next level.**"**

Dan Lin, Producer

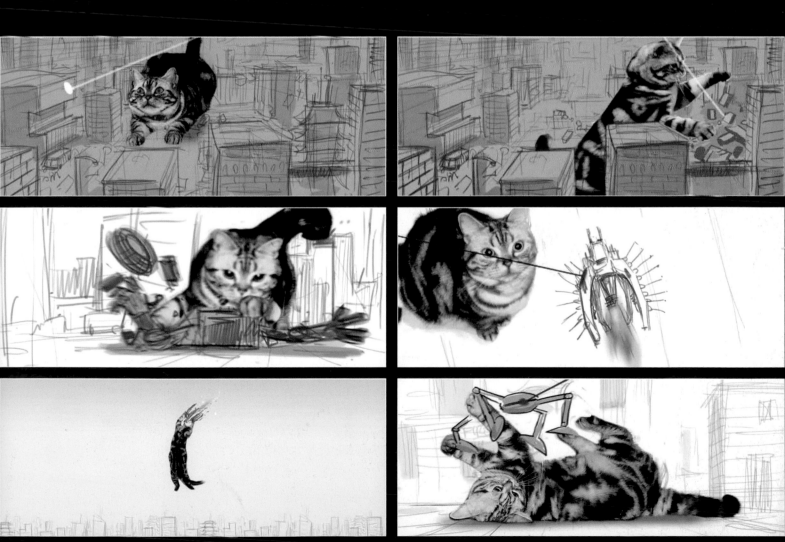

5. STYLING THE MOVIE

Early in the development of the film, Director Charlie Bean knew he wanted to portray the framework of a live-action setting. "With this in mind, we knew that our main new challenge for this film would be to create natural objects and environments at LEGO scale [and] that would have the same realistic feel of a stop-motion film", explains CG Supervisor Greg Jowle. The creative team studied familiar household plants so they would be recognisable "but when seen from a minifigure's perspective, they would take on the aspect of wild jungle foliage, just as they would in a child's imagination", adds Production Designer Kim Taylor.

Small and even smaller · *Development work, Kim Taylor* · Seedlings, moss and other naturally small plants work well as jungle foliage. These small plants were chosen specially for their ability to suit a minifigure-world scale.

A walk in the wild · The design team studied micro plants through extensive macro photo shoots, picturing what a minifigure would see in the great outdoors.

> **"**Every plant in the film is based on a real plant and is modelled to scale. Many of our plants are less than one centimetre high.**"**
>
> **Kim Taylor, Production Designer**

Grapple in the grass • A battle in photo-real moss (and mirco plants found growing within moss) makes it look like combat in the jungle when considered from a minifigure perspective.

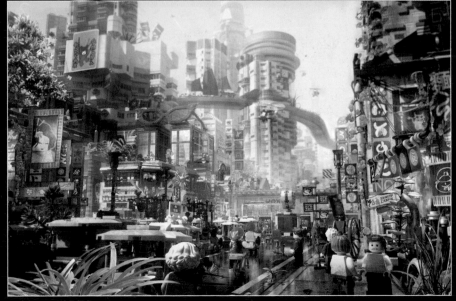

Greening up the city • *Concept art, Michael Halford* • Plant life appears in most shots of the city, to both soften the set built of plastic but also to remind the audience that the greater framework could be a live-action setting or someone's imagination.

6. PRODUCTION DESIGN

Ninjago City is designed with an Asian-influenced aesthetic, as if interpreted through someone else's imaginat. For example, the city has buildings built on top of buildings – LEGO "clutch power" allows for such construction – with both ancient and modern structures intermixed. As for characters, minifigures maintain a LEGO shape while their personalities emerge in creatively varied costume choices and hairstyles. In order to enrich the Ninjago culture, production design even encompassed the development of an entire written language, like calligraphy in appearance yet founded in LEGO shapes – as if it were a secret code.

> **"**Garmadon was a really fun character to build on as he is such an expressive, charismatic bad guy and with the red eyes and four arms he has a very unique look.**"**
>
> **Kim Taylor, Production Designer**

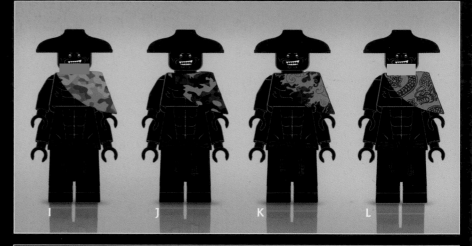

Character crafting • *Concept art, Fiona Darwin and Gibson Radsavanh (top), Djordje Djordjevic (middle)* • Artists, such as Djordje Djordjevic (bottom), created thousands of images for character and location development. Animal Logic and the LEGO Group worked together on many iterations for a single costume, set or prop.

7. ATTENTION TO DETAIL

"Every character, environment, set piece and prop we design could be built in real life because they obey the rules of the LEGO system, working within the colour palette and style guide supplied", notes Animal Logic Art Director Felicity Coonan. Careful attention is paid to the tiniest of details on characters and props, a nod to the fact that LEGO bricks are played with and subject to dirt and scratches, and fingerprints. Meanwhile, environments are presented in natural lighting to reflect the framework of this Ninjago world existing in a real-world setting.

Colour code · The Art Direction team establishes a colourscript of small paintings from important moments in the film to map out the palette progression for each sequence. This ensures that the intended action and emotion of each sequence is supported by its visual impression.

8. FINDING A VOICE

The characters really come alive once they are given their voice. The voice artists are given script pages to follow, but once they get comfortable in their LEGO persona, they will often improvise to bring unexpected humour and emotion to scenes. Editor Julie Rogers spends thousands of hours listening to and cutting voice tracks, and she says she "falls a little bit in love with each of the characters – not just the good guys, but the bad guys as well". Good casting invites the audience to do the same, connecting with the characters as they embark on their on-screen adventures.

Channelling their characters · With Dave Franco (above left) as Green Ninja Lloyd, Justin Theroux (above right) as Lord Garmadon and Jackie Chan (left) as Master Wu, Ninjago City has plenty of character.

9.RESEARCH AND DEVELOPMENT

For research and development work, teams reached into various corners of the world for preparation on this film. Artists took walks in the woods to study micro plants and on the beach to study sand; they watched martial arts and kaiju movies to absorb the feel of these classic film genres; they sought information about Asian design, architecture and symbols in order to craft the Ninjago culture and language; they created new software to support foliage propagation in the film; and of course, they worked with bricks to come up with the coolest characters, sets and mechs imaginable. Simon Lucas describes one of the many processes undergone at the LEGO Group in Billund: "When we need lots of ideas and models made we do something called a "Design Boost". This is where we gather lots of model, graphic and element designers from around the company and we all work together in building cool new concept models. The variety of the models is always fantastic and often there are some standout concepts that end up defining the visual style of a bad guy or new vehicle".

Brick by brick · LEGO designers, such as Luis F. E. Castaneda, Li-Yu Lin and Christopher Leslie Stamp (above), work through mech builds, utilising the plethora of historic LEGO bricks and occasionally moulding new pieces.

Physical and photo check · *Photo, Madeleine Purdy* · Artists at Animal Logic compare actual LEGO builds with how they look "in action" on screen.

10. BUILDING THE CITY

Modelling characters, sets, props and mechs for a LEGO movie is a unique filmmaking task. It is vital to the artistic team "that everything that is meant to be built in LEGO form is assembled brick by brick, the way it would be physically built", explains CG Supervisor Greg Jowle. At last count, the brick library contained nearly 3,000 unique pieces including new bricks that were moulded to create custom wigs for some characters as well as weapons, tools and a few decorative elements. The scope of Ninjago City is enormous and so full of detailed models that "at one point, it grew so large and complex that we had to put a hold on expanding it further until our technology could catch up and allow us to render it", recalls Modelling Supervisor Bradley Sick.

Mech inspect • *Photo, Madeleine Purdy* • Artists consider how mech and set work together with regard to scale and range of motion.

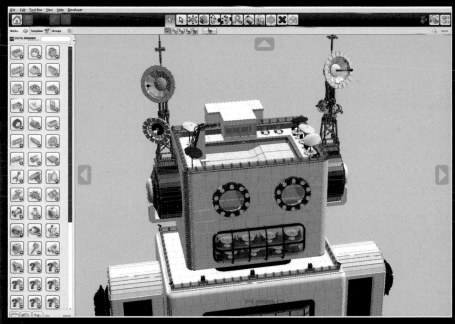

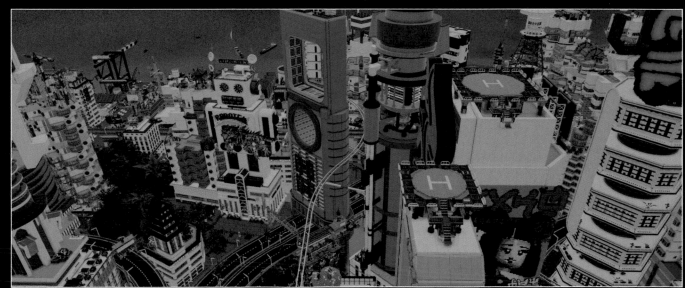

Robotel review • *Design work, Pierre Salazar* • One of the many unique structures in Ninjago City, the Robotel retains minifigure shape while having been modelled up in scale and detail to encompass a luxury high-rise resort.

11. ADDING MOVEMENT

The Rigging team works on all models that need to move in the film, giving them controls for animators to use. "LEGO rigging is actually more complex than it might look at first. Minifigures have realistic ranges of motion, so we don't allow any bending or flexing of the plastic. But we do need to recreate all the complex ways you can animate a figure", explains Rigging Lead Josh Murtack. Of course, when the character or mech is a multi-jointed dragon, the number of pieces involved lends itself to all manner of bending, manipulation and motion.

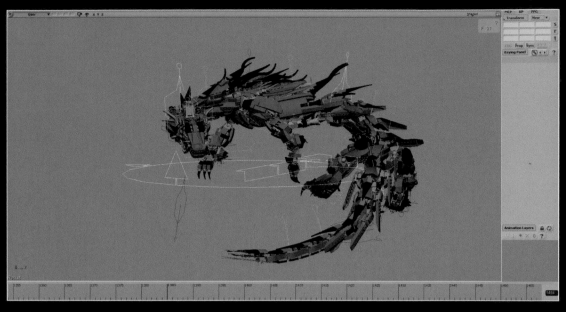

Mech-tacular • The Green Ninja's Dragon Mech is a complicated build, but certainly fun for the Rigging team to manage, as it has many moveable points of connection.

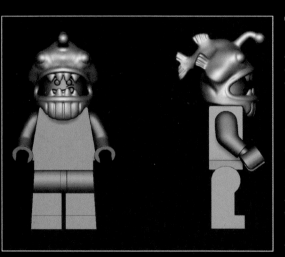

12. LOOKING THE PART

All models require the work of the look development group in order to technically achieve a desired look. A lot of engineering work goes into deciding how a decal might sit upon a minifigure's torso, for example, so that a minifigure does not remain a flat and grey render. Look development for the sets in Ninjago City was more complicated than in previous LEGO films due to the photorealistic jungle setting. "Given that everything is of a miniature scale, the environment surfacing had to be meticulously detailed", explains Look Development Supervisor JP LeBlanc. To support the look of the massive amount of foliage in this film, the Animal Logic team even wrote their own software – a tree-building tool called Spruce and a propagation tool called Spawn.

Shining a light • The Shark Army's Angler Fish soldier went through several stages of development, with designers, such as Nicholas Timothy Whitmore (bottom left) and Niels Milan Pedersen (bottom right), working from blank form to fully moulded, textured minifigure.

13. LEVELLING UP

The layout team translates the story panels into virtual movie sets by putting together actual character, set and prop models in a space with camera angles and camera movements intact. Their work also helps establish a sense of scale, which is important in a LEGO environment. Layout also plans out the need for matte paintings, which are many in Ninjago City due to the number of grand natural sets. "In the background mountains and jungles, we painted large-leafed plants that could not exist in reality", recalls Matte Painting Lead Dudley Birch.

14. A VIRTUAL WORLD

Later in the production pipeline, at the virtual cinematography stage, a "stereographic pass" is taken to add depth and give shots an enriched, more immersive feel. Switching between a live-action world and LEGO sets, and switching between wide angle and long lenses, makes creating an even look more challenging. Use of stereo "helps guide the audience's point of interest... which is important when there is so much visual information to take in: high-contrast shapes and edges, saturated colours, fast cuts, stop-motion animation and the lack of motion blur", explains Stereoscopic Supervisor Fabian Müller.

Four-eyed and sharp-eyed · *Photo, Madeleine Purdy* · The team reviews the film in stereoscopic playback to make sure the use of depth of camera adds to the cinematic experience and does not distract from it.

Lights, camera, action · Layout images show various camera set-ups in a single frame of action, giving filmmakers a choice of perspective for shots.

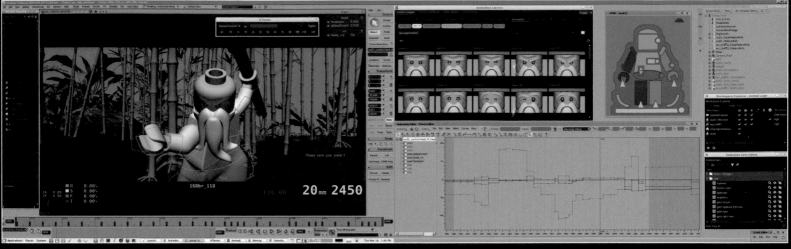

15. READY FOR ACTION

The animation team has the incredible task of making rigid models move in a fluid, believable way and express themselves enough to connect with an audience. "Getting the hard plastic characters to emote probably seems more challenging than it is, but in a way, the simple iconic aspect of their faces makes their expressions easier to relate to", notes Director Charlie Bean. Animators study the backstory, likes, dislikes and idiosyncrasies of their characters "in order to create how they walk, stand, sit, talk and look at each other and the world," explains Animation Director Matt Everitt. At the same time, the animators respect the LEGO medium, not giving characters the typical "squash and stretch" treatment when in motion, but instead swapping out pieces over the course of a frame to replicate a change in shape that a motion blur effect would accomplish in more traditional animation mediums.

Kung-fu master of the medium • Master Wu is voiced by Jackie Chan, who influenced not only his character through voice performance, but also by helping choreograph his martial arts moves.

"When you start working on a LEGO project, you expect to be constrained by what you can and can't do with a set number of bricks shapes and styles. With each LEGO film, we are continuing to find that there are so many fun and ingenious ways to achieve the visual or emotional beat while still staying true to the LEGO spirit."

Ingrid Johnston, Head of Production

ANIMATING MEOWTHRA

Since THE LEGO NINJAGO MOVIE takes place in the framework of the real world, there are certain live-action-seeming elements that carry onto the big screen, with the most challenging being the cat also known as Meowthra. The production had originally thought to film a live-action cat for all of these scenes, but a computer-generated version was also crafted since it could take better direction. "Since our virtual Meowthra had to replicate a live cat that was specifically cast for the film, it required new development in fur grooming tools as well as photorealistic shading", explains Look Development Supervisor JP LeBlanc. This furball contained approximately nine million hairs and required a whole team of artists to generate the purr-fect destructive, yet adorable, monster.

Curiosity filmed the cat · The actor gets his close-up, and gets to know his co-star – a LEGO mech – as well.

zad01_cat_action08   F 5.60   50 mm 1124

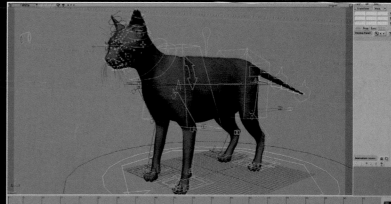

zad01_cat_action09   F 5.60   50 mm 1155

Green screen to film the scene · Directing the live-action cat and matching his movement and silhouette with a CG-replication was the most organic and non-brick process in the making of the film.

Fake fur · Masterful digital artistry brings Meowthra to life.

16. SPECIAL EFFECTS

"From the start, the Creative team pushed all the effects to become non-brick based. This push came because the Ninjago environment was a natural world containing trees, plants, soil, sand and oceans, therefore it seemed right that all the effects became natural, too", explains Effects Supervisor Miles Green. The use of photo-real natural environmental effects comes with a set of challenges unique to this film, all related to making them integrate with LEGO elements in a charming, believable way. The look of everything underwater or wet required special attention from effects, look development, and lighting artists. On top of that, water simulation takes a tidal wave of computer processing memory, which puts a heavy load on the rendering department.

It's elemental · *Concept art (left), Yannick Tan; animation development (above)* · Mixing LEGO elements with natural elements such as as water, fire and sand adds interesting layers of work to many departments. The effects team used watering cans and fish tanks to investigate water effects on LEGO pieces. They burnt paper and small candles to study smoke and flame on a small scale, and walked along the beach to study sand and foam on the shore. "A word of warning: minifigures are easily swept out to sea!" as Miles Green, Effects Supervisor, can attest.

17. GOING UP IN LIGHTS

The Ninjago world is lit so that it looks as much like a real LEGO environment under physical lighting conditions, "with a generally upbeat aesthetic", explains Lighting Supervisor Craig Welsh. The artistic team aims for "naturation" – their term for natural saturation of colour – so that it looks like it was photographed by expert miniature cinematographers in the real world. It is the task of lighting artists to direct the audience's eye, a particular challenge in a world as busy and colourful as Ninjago City. "We accomplish this by shaping the way light falls in the scene, maybe putting characters in dramatic rim light and playing them against a shadowed background; or by using atmospheric effects to help silhouette the action, such as having smoke or mist build up with distance", Welsh adds.

Now you see him · The lighting team must ensure that the audience can see the character at all times, no matter how busy the background, ambient light or effects are within a frame.

Trading focus for fuzz • Optical effects are what allow background elements to fall out of focus and a bit of lens grit to appear in shots, giving both visual interest and direction to the audience's eye.

18. A BALANCING ACT

All visual elements come together in a perfect balance crafted by the compositing and rendering work. "In short, compositing takes clean and perfect CG renders and beats them up enough to look real. By adding all the errors and optical imperfections we see in real physical lenses, we make the image more beautiful by making it objectively "worse"", explains Compositing Supervisor Alex Fry. By applying a variety of optical effects, the compositing team layers in lens flare, image defocus, lens breathing and other desired visual alteration by using photographic elements shot with vintage Panavision lenses. It was particularly fun for the compositing team to grant Director Charlie Bean's wish to incorporate throwback 1980s video effects to emulate the gritty look of Hong Kong cinema: "we push the image around to evoke the vibe of long-dead cinema technologies, whilst avoiding the grim reality of actually using them", adds Fry.

19. EDITING

The editing team works throughout the entire animation pipeline, starting with the creation of the story panel animatic, updating shots as each department finishes its work, and finessing the cut along the way. Editorial is particularly helpful in efficiently creating alternate versions of how important scenes might play out: for instance, Editor Julie Rogers recalls "wrestling with a lot of versions of the opening few scenes to try to find a balance of entertainment, exposition, and connection to Lloyd". This team sets the pacing, continuity, and tone of the film through its use of different cinematic techniques as well as temporary music and sound effects. "Action sequences often utilize quick cuts and moving cameras to give a sense of energy and make the viewer feel off balance, while comedy is frequently flatter and more succinct in its look and pacing", says Rogers.

Always watching and refining • *Photo, Madeleine Purdy* • The editorial team spends countless hours watching and rewatching scenes and sequences as they build the movie from story panels all the way to final frames.

20. SCORING A HIT

Once the visuals are locked, focus shifts to the sound needs of the film. Sound effects are layered to create a broader sensory experience – wind rustling in jungle foliage, distant waves crashing along a shore or heavy breathing to name just a few audible accessories. Temporary music is replaced by final score and/or songs to give the film a more cohesive through-line for emotion and pacing – and might even leave audience members singing a memorable tune as they leave the cinemas!

Musical metaphors · Sound and music enriches the cinematic experience with melody and other auditory cues.

21. THE FINAL CUT

The ultimate stop for all elements in the filmmaking pipeline is the final mix, where picture and sound come together in perfect alignment to satisfy the needs of big-screen projection. Colour may have to be adjusted, sound elements may have to be played up or down and stereoscopic influence may have to be increased or decreased – whatever it takes to provide an enjoyable cinematic experience.

All eyes and ears attuned · Great attention is paid to every aspect of the film in the final mix because filmmakers want to make sure their hard work is conveyed in the desired manner to their audience. Here, Tim LeBlanc works on the WB sound stage.

Minifigure madness • Artists and designers, such as Lars Roersen Nielsen and Djordje Djordjevic (above), enjoy making minifigures for both the big screen and real-world play, especially if they can put an evil warlord in cute pyjamas.

22. NINJA-GO!

Perhaps the best part about a LEGO film experience is that it doesn't have to end once audiences leave the cinema. Instead, it can be re-enacted or reinterpreted by fans around the world when they bring physical models into their own homes. "My favourite part of THE LEGO NINJAGO MOVIE is the mix of the natural world and LEGO bricks. It reminds me of being a kid, taking my LEGO sets out into the garden and making my own stories. I really hope that this movie inspires kids to do the same", says Simon Lucas, LEGO Senior Creative Director.

Mechs and more • Simon Lucas, Senior Creative Director at the LEGO Group, loves that he plays with toys as a career, but more so that he can share these amazing models with fans of all ages around the globe.

"I hope kids take the message about achieving your greatest potential to heart, realising that once you accept yourself, you will find your true inner strength.**"**

Maryann Garger, Producer

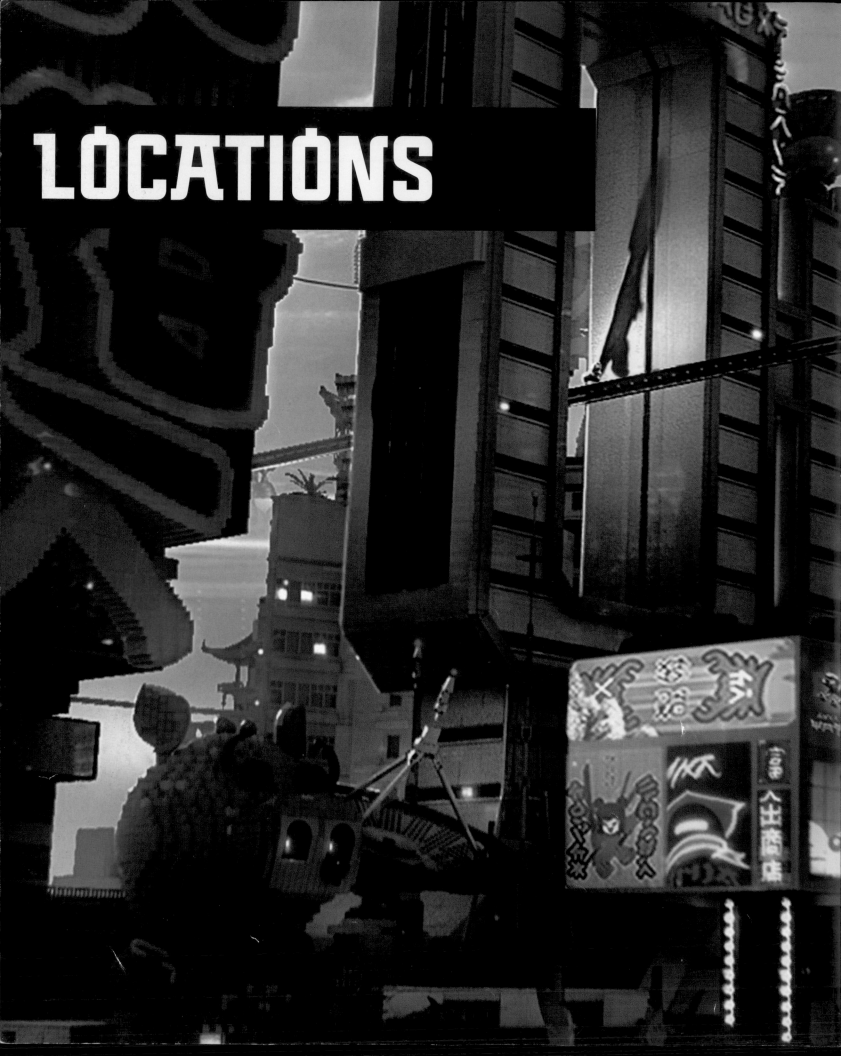

LOCATIONS

NINJAGO® CITY

Ninjago® City exists on the edge of an island, but it is truly in its own world. As far as anyone knows, there are no other cities, countries, or communities beyond it. This thriving metropolis is a mix of old and new structures, richly inspired by Asian design elements. It is the ultimate creative environment, with its own unique culture, characteristics and other fun details that could only spring forth in an imaginative LEGO® world.

Old and new, low and high · *Concept art, Adam Ryan and Kim Taylor* · Ninjago City is characterised by a rich sense of history and energy, with ancient buildings co-existing alongside skyscrapers, and traditional wood structures beneath modern electric railways. This black-and-white image was one of the first concept images that helped the film get its green light into production.

Island paradise and population · *Concept art, Heiko Drengenberg and Joe Feinsilver (right), Dudley Birch (below)* · Aerial views show a scene of beauty and isolation around Ninjago City, establishing the location as an unexpected structural gem in the surrounding nature. The island's shape represents a yin and yang symbol, displaying contrasting energies in balance.

NINJAGO CITY

Standing tall • *Concept art, Michael Halford* • Early work such as this sought to establish a unique skyline for Ninjago City. This image, with its silhouette of great visual interest and an intriguing mix of shapes and details, inspired further work in this direction.

CITY HIGHRISES

The sky's the limit... or not really, in a LEGO brick-built city. Gravity and standard engineering rules do not apply in this imaginative space, so highrises can reach amazing heights and styles in Ninjago City.

Everything old is new again • *Concept art, Mark Sexton (top left), Peter Commins (bottom left)* • The early village-like settlement of this LEGO community morphed upward into a modern cityscape.

Oh, the places you'll see · *Concept art, Peter Commins and Kim Taylor* · Only in a LEGO world would designers imagine buildings shaped like gorillas, or offset stacks of blocks that only work because of the LEGO system of locking bricks.

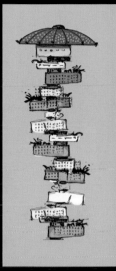

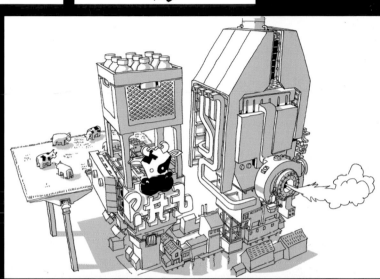

Alphabet architecture · *Concept art, Yannick Tan* · LEGO structures can spell out words in their design (see pages 44–45 to decode).

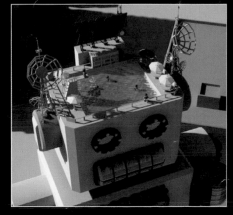

Hi-tech resort · *Concept art, Pierre Salazar* · A robot-shaped hotel – the Robotel – offers a rooftop pool and relaxing space as part of its modern hotel amenities.

MODERN SKYLINE

As beautiful as the natural island around it is, modern-day Ninjago City is a feast for the eyes with all its detail and colour. Asian and LEGO influence on fun and modern architecture can be seen in every inch of this cityscape.

"From the first concepts I painted, I knew this needed to be a unique city where imagination triumphed over instructions every time."

Kim Taylor, Production Designer

Then and now · *Concept art, Kim Taylor (top), Peter Commins and Michael Halford (above), Peter Commins (below)* · The direct comparison of a particular perspective from long ago and today's Ninjago City shows a few notable holdover landmarks – and a lot of new construction around them.

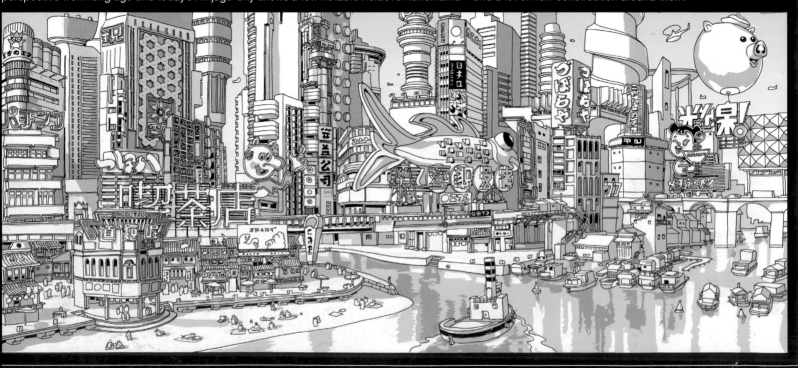

A city of dreams • *Concept art, Peter Commins* • These black-and-white and colour designs and ideas added much to Ninjago City's whimsical chaos.

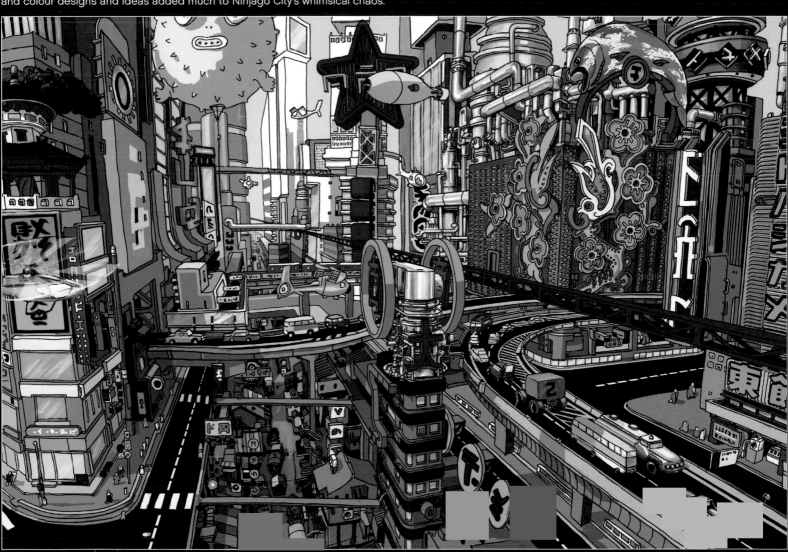

Aglow with activity · *Final render* ·
Energy radiates from Ninjago City at
all hours of the day and night. With its
charming luminescence, it draws the
audience into wanting to see what
the hustle and bustle is all about.

Graced by green • *Concept art, Michael Halford* • Plant life fits around the elements of the busy city. The plants look real because they are! Genuine shrubbery and leaves were used to create the effect.

CITYSCAPES

Ninjago City has been built up into a modern-day bustling city, However, it still retains some of its old-world charm and natural features with a mix of wooden structures, greenery and waterways woven throughout.

A view of the open sea • *Concept art, Yannick Tan* • The wide vista of Ninjago City's waterfront section adds relaxing scenery. The rippling surface gives a glimpse of the seabed beneath.

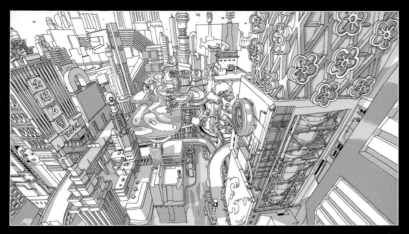

Growing green • *Concept art, Peter Commins* • The transformation from line-drawing concept to layout model image shows the golf course as a bright spot in a city setting. These development processes are par for the course in this film's development.

The puff appears • *Concept art, Yannick Tan and Kim Taylor* • Set dressing and the fine tuning of colour and lighting creates a rich visual tone for the busy environment – flying fish included.

Building the Robotel • *Concept art, Yannick Tan* • As the development work progresses, details on buildings, light streaming through the city and water in the canal come into focus. Here, the Robotel marches straight into the foreground.

NINJAGO CITY MODELS

LEGO designers have one of the best jobs in the world – playing with their imagination and some really cool materials every day. Some amazing multi-level builds came out of a "boost session" of brainstorm building, putting creativity on top of creativity to construct a truly layered Ninjago City model.

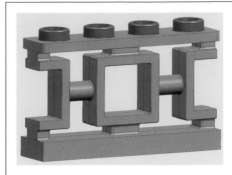

Brick-tastic · LEGO *model development, Esa Petteri Nousiainen, Nicolaas Vás, Christopher Stamp ·* LEGO designers generally try to work within the vast realm of already-made bricks, but when they have a chance to make a new piece, it is something special, such as this fence detail for use in Ninjago City.

Early phases · LEGO *model development, Nicolaas Vás, Niek Duco van Slagmaat ·* These two early versions of the Ninjago City set played with the size and scope of multiple layers being stacked on top of one another. Here, there's much more than meets the eye inside as well as outside, including THE LEGO® MOVIE™ star Wyldstyle scaling the rooftop sushi bar (left).

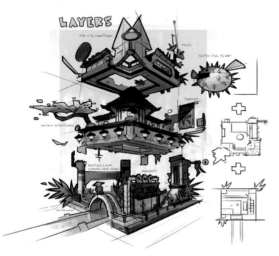

> "Ninjago City is a crazy LEGO metropolis full of characters – even some you might recognise from other LEGO themes."

Simon Lucas, LEGO Senior Creative Director

Layer by layer • *Concept art, Matt Betteker* • These images illustrate how the multiple levels of a Ninjago City building fit together, with Lloyd's apartment on top and the canal down below.

A model home, and then some • *LEGO model development, Nicolaas Vás, Christopher Stamp* • The final build has countless fun details in its construct, from fun fish signage on top, to Secret Ninja Force action figures in the comic shop and sewer snakes swimming down below.

Natural overlook • *Final render* • At dusk or dawn – or anytime in between that they are not in school – the Secret Ninja Force is on watch over Ninjago City. In fact, although Green Ninja Lloyd looks like he's standing on a faraway hill, this microscale version of the city is only a metre away from him!

for a martial arts movie, and the contrast of LEGO [bricks] and nature is really beautiful. **"**

Charlie Bean, Director

NINJAGO LANGUAGE

Before audiences can fully appreciate Ninjago City, they must first recognise that the culture has developed its own writing system, known as Ninjago Language. To create this alphabet, designers crafted letters and numerals that appear Asian in style, yet are based on the symbols of the Latin alphabet. Characters can be used vertically, horizontally, or in pictogram clusters. This language allows for countless fun inside jokes if audiences take the time to decode it.

Script sculpting • *Graphic art, Felicity Coonan* • Art Director Felicity Coonan started by looking at oddly shaped and rare LEGO pieces that vaguely represented letters. She then reinterpreted them by drawing them freehand and slowly refining their shapes through these iterations of the Ninjago Language.

Big and bold • *Graphic art, Felicity Coonan* • While a brush style of script is good for more ancient signage, modern businesses required cleaner fonts, which is what this alphabet represents: in both its letters and its numbers.

"Master"

"Play well"

"Rice and shine"

"Yum yum"

"Moo", "stick",
"kebab"

"Miso"

Master Wu's tags

J	K	L	M	N	O	P	Q	R

1	2	3	4	5	6	7	8	9

CITY SIGNAGE

In a community as busy as Ninjago City, retail and services abound on every street corner and on many stories above. To that end, the need for appealing signage gave the design team an opportunity to play with Ninjago Language on many levels, literally and graphically speaking.

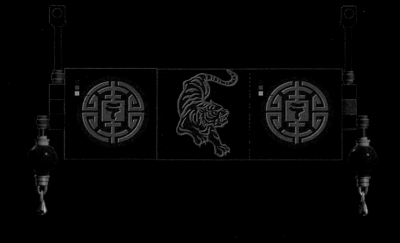

"Much of this graphic work is centred around the aesthetic of kung-fu films and anime, but we also did a lot of research into Asian architecture and design."

Felicity Coonan, Art Director

As far as the eye can see (and the wallet can reach) · *Concept art, Takumer Homma* · In some views of Ninjago City, the commercial areas create lots of business for the audience's eye, thanks to vibrant and vast signage.

SHRIMP CAKES

Condishiwig

Shine that will last forever

Now available at your local **PRICEYPLEASE +**

BEAN DUMPLINGS

SUSHI

HE KNOCKS IT DOWN WE BUILD IT UP

NINJAGO CITY
MASTER RE-BUILDERS ASSOCIATION

Business is good – and graphically appealing · *Concept art, Felicity Coonan, Jessica Sommerville, Fiona Darwin, Gibson Radsavanh and Pierre Salazar* · There are so many commerce options in Ninjago City, with so many tantalising signs advertising them, that citizens may never have to visit the same noodle shop or pad-thai booth twice!

SHOP STALLS

The citizens of Ninjago City require many businesses to cover their needs, and thus many plastic bricks were laid to create a bounty of options. Some of the stalls are fixed whereas others, due to the ever-changing nature of the city, have wheels to help them move to where the action is.

Puffer-fish blimp restaurant

Pig blimp restaurant

Market newsstand

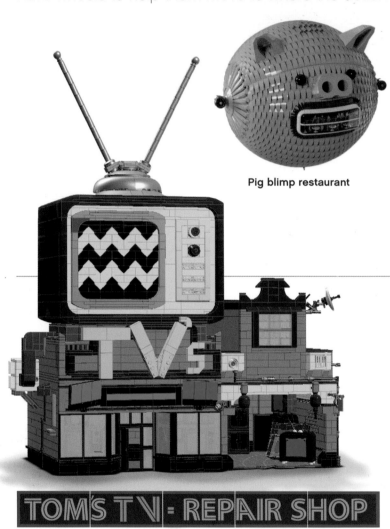

TOM'S TV - REPAIR SHOP

Big screen scene • *Concept art (above), Peter Commins* • In early versions of the story, Zane lived at a TV repair shop, a concept channelled in these images.

Meat needs met here • *Concept art, Pierre Salazar (left), Peter Commins (above)* • Inspired by Chinese butcher shops and Japanese tonkatsu restaurants, these images will satisfy the appetites of hungry carniverous citizens.

Stalls installed · *Final render (left);* LEGO *model development (below and far left)* · The narrow streets provide a busy place of business for some of these stalls. They're surrounded by customers, but also competition, and the occasional cat.

Popcorn cart

Pad-thai-sushi tacos

Noodle cart

Hot-noodle-dog stand

Fabric rug seller

Mochi balls

Shrimp pancakes

FIsh BBQ grill

Spices stand

Fish, fruit and physical model · *LEGO model, Dimitrios Stamatis* · This lucky street vendor has had his stall made into a physical LEGO model in connection with the feature film. Covering two important food groups – fish and fruit – in one booth apparently makes good business and brick sense!

LLOYD'S APARTMENT

Ninjago City packs so much into so little space, and Lloyd's apartment is a prime example of such efficiency. One of thousands of small compartments in which people live in this community, Lloyd's home contains all the basic comforts needed by mother and son, with a bit of LEGO fun thrown in.

Luminescent laundry and lodgings · *Final render* · Apartment living in Ninjago City may be tight on space, but its inhabitants enjoy good lighting when there's a full moon.

Home in a box · *Animation development* · Modular living such as these apartment buildings is perfectly logical and efficient, and all the more so in a LEGO environment.

Setting the table · *Storyboard image (above), Natalie Wetzig; LEGO models (right); decal, Felicity Coonan* · These are the very first spoon and bowls moulded for the LEGO world – or else Lloyd would never have been able to enjoy his morning bowl of cereal!

Cozy yet complete · *Concept art, Simon Whiteley* · This overhead view of the entire apartment shows just how much detail can be squeezed into a small space.

Bed space and head space · *Final render (above); graphic artwork (below), Fiona Darwin and Felicity Coonan* · When Lloyd lays himself down to sleep, posters and books echoing real-world kung-fu movies are nearby to inspire his dreams and secret life of being a ninja.

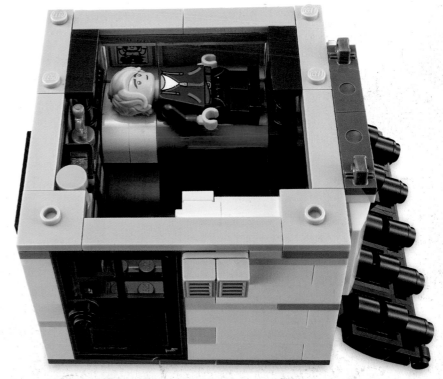

Tucked in tight · *LEGO model* · The physical model of Lloyd's bedroom shows just how compact a compartment it truly is. But there is still room for bunk beds and also for Lloyd's action figures and books.

The bell is about to ring • *Colourscript image (above), Takumer Homma; final render (left)* • Ninjago High School is a relatively modern, yet definitely institutional style of building. For most students, it is a warm and welcoming environment. An early concept image even featured a friendly statue at the entrance of two clasped minifigure hands.

NINJAGO HIGH SCHOOL

When Lloyd and his gang are not in ninja mode, they are regular students at Ninjago High School. One has to wonder if their teachers grow suspicious of their repeated requests for bathroom absences when Lord Garmadon comes to town.

All aboard • *LEGO model development, Kristen Anderson* • The school bus is inspired by a classic American school bus, eclectically decorated with signs and decorations.

Class posters ·
Graphic art, Felicity Coonan · Classroom instruction posters include the periodic table of elements and a skeleton diagram, as translated into the world of LEGO colours and minifigures. Labels are added in Ninjago Language.

In the classroom · *Concept art, Tim Pyman* · Modelling supervisor Bradley Sick was inspired by the traditional American high school building he attended for this early development image. This sparsely furnished and slightly shabby look was quickly agreed upon.

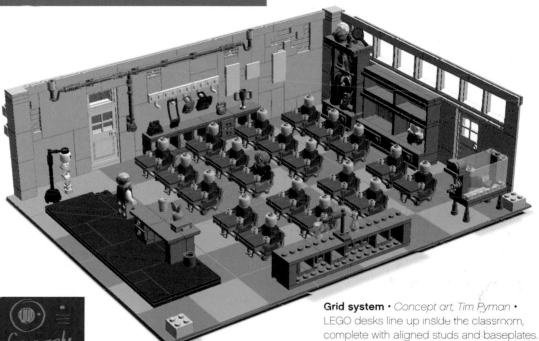

Grid system · *Concept art, Tim Pyman* · LEGO desks line up inside the classroom, complete with aligned studs and baseplates.

Mr Peterson professes · *Concept art. Gibson Radsavanh* · The Ninjago High School teacher presents his social studies lessons on a traditional blackboard. Designers experimented with what messages could be read with the blind alternately up and down.

A hallway unto himself · *Colourscript image, Kim Taylor* · Lloyd wanders through long, empty corridors that echo his isolated mindset. A missing ceiling panel here and there represents how he is falling apart because of the never-ending mocking about his evil father.

In session · *Colourscript image, Kim Taylor* · While most of the
Ninjago High students have nothing to worry about apart from
concentrating on the lesson at hand, the Secret Ninja Force

"High school is generally a tough time for everyone, going through lots of different emotions and issues of self-identity, but for Lloyd it is extra challenging, with his father being who he is. "

Dan Lin, Producer

NINJAGO HIGH STUDENTS AND TEACHERS

As much as he thinks all eyes are on him, it's not always about Lloyd in the busy public high school. His fellow secret ninja each face their own challenges in this bustling, youthful environment.

School pride • *Graphic art, Felicity Coonan* • The motto of Ninjago High is "Stick Together", which is easier to accomplish with studs and baseplates than with a bunch of awkwardly insensitive teenagers.

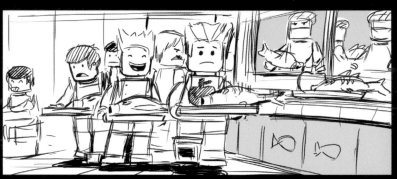

Tough times • *Concept art, Donald Walker (top), Kim Taylor and Chris Reccardi (above)* • From dating to grades to embarrassing clothing mishaps, even the ninja must battle the trials and tribulations of being a teenager.

Student bodies • *Concept art, Nadia Attlee, Fiona Darwin, Felicity Coonan, and Gibson Radsavanh* • Just like any good high-school movie, classmates at Ninjago High School cover all walks of life and iconic fashion.

Teacher trio • *Concept art, Nadia Attlee, Fiona Darwin, Djordje Djordjevic* • A few of the staff members educate the audience on what a typical teacher might look like in the realm of minifigures.

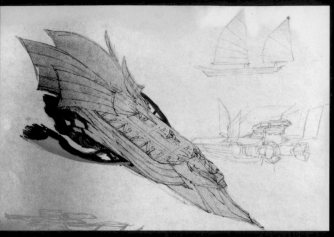

DESTINY'S BOUNTY

Home base for Master Wu and his dojo is a large ship in the harbour of Ninjago City, a three-masted paddle-wheeler named *Destiny's Bounty* that is more publicly recognised as a tea barge. Designs for this ship ranged from rustic to modern, with and without the ability to fly, but always with a ninja-training facility within its hull.

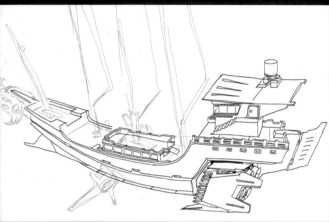

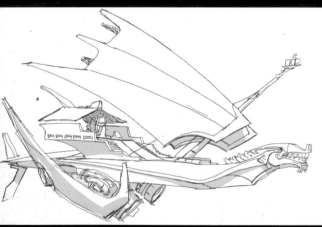

Afloat with imagination · *Concept art, Vaughan Ling and Peter Commins* · Earliest versions of the ship portrayed a more futuristic look… because anything cool and new is "so ninja," as the Secret Ninja Force likes to point out from time to time.

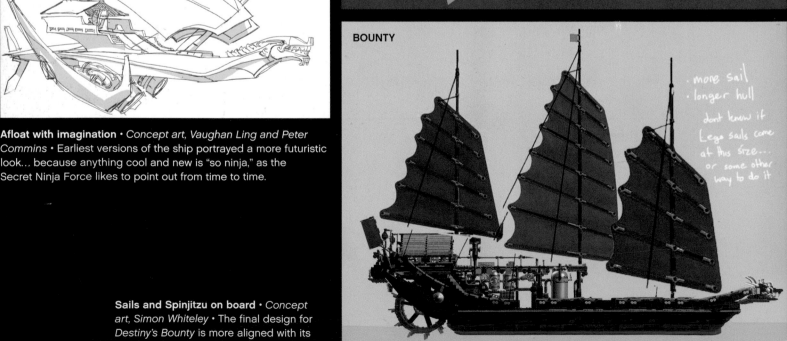

BOUNTY

more sail
longer hull
dont know if Lego sails come at this size… or some other way to do it

Sails and Spinjitzu on board · *Concept art, Simon Whiteley* · The final design for Destiny's Bounty is more aligned with its build for the LEGO NINJAGO: *Masters of Spinjitzu* TV series, which fans know has worked well for the ninja in the past.

"*Destiny's Bounty* is such an iconic part of the Ninjago universe. The movie gave us the opportunity to re-imagine how it might look on the big screen.**"**

Simon Lucas, LEGO Senior Creative Director

Unassuming headquarters • *Concept art, Takumer Homma* • The fog-filled harbour casts an air of mystery around *Destiny's Bounty* – no one would suspect what innovative training takes place on the understated ship.

On deck • *Concept art, Charles Santoso, Gibson Radsavanh* • The dock location of *Destiny's Bounty* sets the scene for ninja training in a less hectic, more peaceful space outside of Ninjago City proper.

Training in progress • *Concept art, Gibson Radsavanh* • Master Wu bestows his wisdom to the ninja inside the training dojo on board *Destiny's Bounty*.

Tools of the trade • *Animation development* • The ship carries many tools and gadgets required in the training of ninja, including a hard-core yet plastic-built fighting mannequin.

Treasure trove • LEGO *model development, Christopher Stamp* • Master Wu's sleeping quarters, and various cabins below deck on this early LEGO build, reveal throwbacks to LEGO NINJAGO television villains. Snake staffs and other artifacts make for pleasing "Easter eggs."

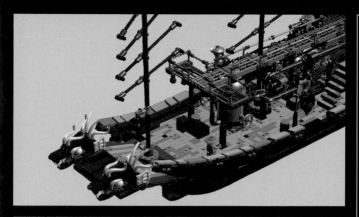

Fierce front pieces

• LEGO *model development,
Nicolaas Vás, Michael Svane Knap* •
LEGO designers explored a variety
of dragon-head designs for the
figureheads of *Destiny's Bounty*.
Using different bricks, they sought to
achieve the same fierce expression
on both a large and a smaller scale.

Time for tea • *Concept art, Simon Whiteley* • Designers spent a
great deal of time and focus on developing both the mechanics
and the appeal of the ship, making sure it was worthy of its noble
ninja cause. This concept explored the idea of Wu having his
very own tea-brewing machine on board ship.

SEA-WORTHY

• LEGO *model, Christopher
Stamp* • The final physical model
of *Destiny's Bounty* is a sight to
behold in its full-sailed glory,
complete with dragon details
and Master Wu's emblem. Look
closer and you can see the ninja
going about their daily training
and ninja lives.

NINJA MECH GARAGE

Just down the waterfront from where *Destiny's Bounty* is docked is the warehouse that serves as a garage for the Secret Ninja Force's mechs. Who knew that such a nondescript structure could be hiding such awesome technology?

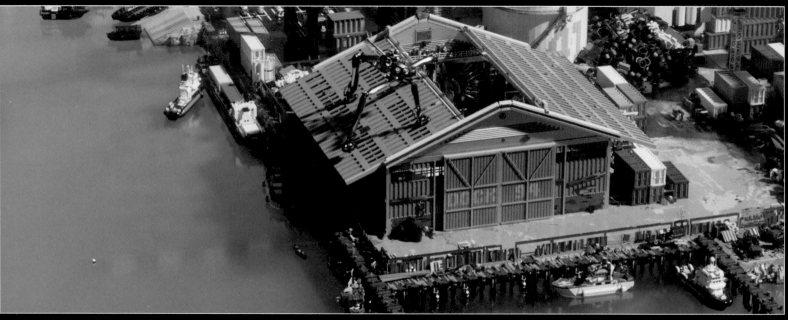

Mega-mecha-parking lot · *Animation development (top); final render (above)* · An aerial shot shown in rough model form gives an overview of the dockside warehouse setting. A colour close-up shows the warehouse's mechanised roof and large sliding doors, which allow mechs various points of entry on their super-sized scale.

Clubhouse code · *Animation development* · The Secret Ninja Force make it clear that no one outside of their inner circle is allowed in their warehouse.

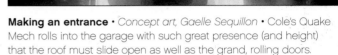

Time to kick back • *Concept art, Jessica Sommerville (right), Felicity Coonan (below); final render (bottom)* • When Kai comes back from a hard day's work fighting Garmadon, his Fire Mech deserves a relaxing recliner rest. These technical drawings reveal how the mech clicks into place and charges back up.

Making an entrance • *Concept art, Gaelle Sequillon* • Cole's Quake Mech rolls into the garage with such great presence (and height) that the roof must slide open as well as the grand, rolling doors.

Chill-out zone • *Animation development* • The garage is also a place where the Secret Ninja Force can relax and unwind. In between battles with Garmadon, they battle each other on retro arcade games!

HIGHSCORES

★ 1	KING-COLE	9997 ★
2	NYA!	9989
3	KILLERKAI	9631
4	KILLERKAI	9030
5	KILLERKAI	9030

BACK

A good night's sleep • *Colourscript image, Yannick Tan* • The mechs power down after a hard day's work protecting the citizens of Ninjago City.

LORD GARMADON'S VOLCANO LAIR

Garmadon has established his home base on a volcanic island off the coast of Ninjago City. The dark, mysterious, fiery and hard-to-access locale is the perfect nest for an evil warlord.

The sharks are circling • *Concept art, Kim Taylor* • The obsidian spikes that surround the lair echo shark fins, adding to the intimidating aura of Garmadon's lair.

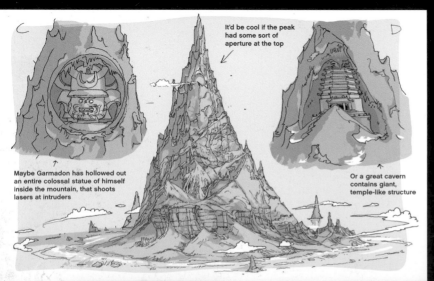

It'd be cool if the peak had some sort of aperture at the top

Maybe Garmadon has hollowed out an entire colossal statue of himself inside the mountain, that shoots lasers at intruders

Or a great cavern contains giant, temple-like structure

No doubt who lives here • *Concept art, Peter Commins* • Having Garmadon's likeness carved into the side of the volcano makes a solid statement about who is master of this domain.

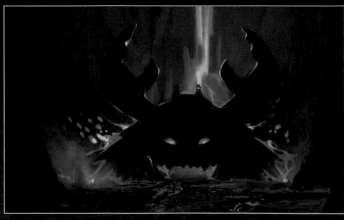

Flare and glare • *Concept art, Kim Taylor* • The use of flame creates a haunting backlight to the likeness of Garmadon that fronts his lair. Entry is via his grimacing mouth opening – a cool feature in this otherwise fiery location.

Ultimate vehicle storage · *Concept art, Peter Commins (above), Gibson Radsavanh (right)* · In a set-up that rivals the Batcave from The LEGO® BATMAN MOVIE, Garmadon's parked fleet rises up into the height of the volcano. At the same time, he can also lower boats down into the ocean below. Many of the mechs have their own specialised docking bays.

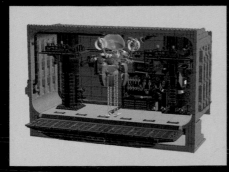

Jelly Sub Bay

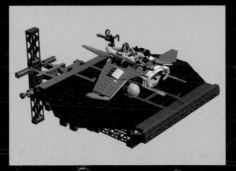

Manta Sub Platform

Large Crab Bay

Fire at will! · *Colourscript image, Gibson Radsavanh and Kim Taylor* · An unhappy employee is escorted out of Command Central upon his dismissal. He will be taken directly to the launching pad where he will be fired out of the volcano top.

CONTROL CENTRE

Command Central houses both the military and technology brains of Garmadon's evil operation. No matter how incredible he thinks he is, Garmadon cannot defeat Ninjago City and those ninja on his own.

Buttons and wires for miles · *Animation development, Jessica Sommerville and Fiona Darwin (top), Simon Whiteley (above)* · The IT nerds have more servers, cords and controls than imaginable in their set-up to serve the needs of Garmadon.

Powerful perch · LEGO *model, Li-Yu Lin* · The set build for Lord Garmadon's Command Central follows the same mountainous shape as the exterior volcano. The lair is complete with a high platform from which Garmadon can loom over everyone, of course.

GARMADON'S BOARDROOM

Big, important discussions happen in Garmadon's big, important boardroom, and it's easy for him to turn up the heat on his generals and tech personnel when there is lava flowing beneath this space.

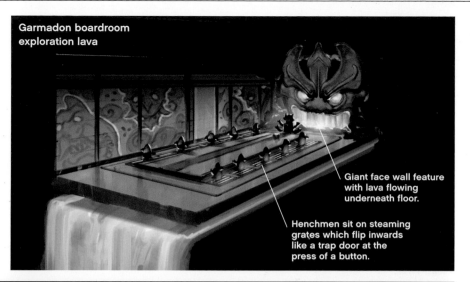

Garmadon boardroom exploration lava

Giant face wall feature with lava flowing underneath floor.

Henchmen sit on steaming grates which flip inwards like a trap door at the press of a button.

Fire, fire everywhere • *Concept art, Gibson Radsavanh and Kim Taylor* • Garmadon likes to see his minions sweat, literally and figuratively. The literal part was explored in an early design – where Garmadon's minions sat on steaming grates that could be flipped over at the press of a button.

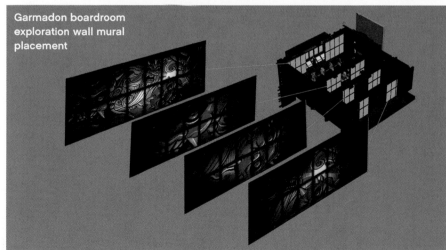

Garmadon boardroom exploration wall mural placement

Artwork is his ally • *Concept art, Gibson Radsavanh* • A large fire-demon face fills the door panels upon entry to the boardroom, setting up all who enter in a proper state of fear and intimidation before they even see Garmadon himself.

Time for a spot of tea • *Graphic art, Felicity Coonan* • Even the most feared warlord has time for a civilised cuppa, and who wouldn't want to sip out of such a beautiful jade-looking LEGO tea set, complete with woodblock-style printing?

Grotesque greeters · *Concept art, Gibson Radsavanh* · These not-so-welcoming faces peer out from the ominous mural in the entryway to Garmadon's boardroom.

NINJAGO BEACH

White sand and clear blue water make for a relaxing beach holiday in Ninjago City... that is, until Garmadon and his Shark Army emerge from the water to cause chaos. Creating this idyllic-looking scene was a challenge for the designers, who combined real-life sand and water with LEGO minifigures.

> "We needed to see and simulate the individual grains of sand from the minifigure perspective, so this meant we were simulating and rendering around 20-80 million grains of sand on a typical shot."
>
> **Miles Green, FX Supervisor**

Shark attack! · *Colourscript image (top), Kim Taylor; final render (above)* · If only that fin were just one shark and not an entire Shark Army announcing their arrival and casting a long shadow across the sand.

Beachy keen · *Concept art, Fiona Darwin* · Innocent beachgoers populate this space, in different styles of bathing suits and with varying amounts of body hair – much like in the real world.

Run for your lives! · *Storyboard art, Januel Mercado* · A progression of story panels in this intense sequence shows not only the action as it builds shot-by-shot, but also colour and detail.

Seaside snack · *Final render* · This beachgoer is barely a mouthful for Lord Garmadon's predatory mech.

NINJAGO TOWER

The tallest, most prominent building in Ninjago City is the Ninjago Tower. Garmadon naturally sees this as the perfect place in which to install his new headquarters after conquering the land. He has his shark-copters uproot his volcanic lair and perch it on top of this structure so that he can keep an eye on his new realm, and so that it will look suitably volcanic and gloomy.

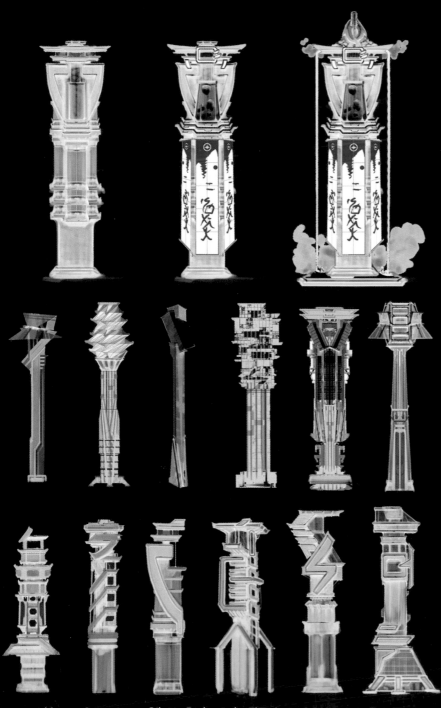

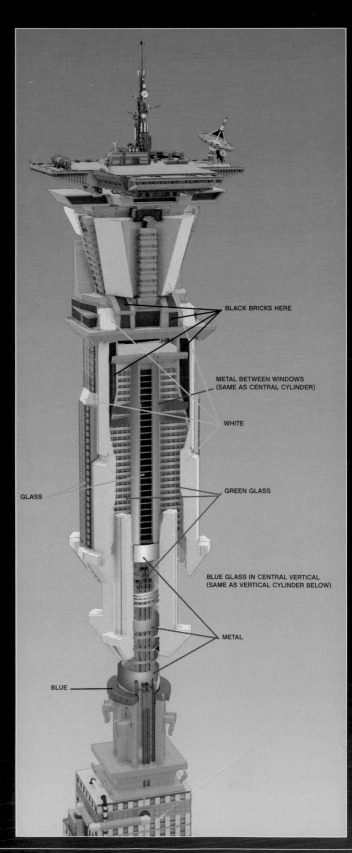

BLACK BRICKS HERE

METAL BETWEEN WINDOWS
(SAME AS CENTRAL CYLINDER)

WHITE

GLASS

GREEN GLASS

BLUE GLASS IN CENTRAL VERTICAL
(SAME AS VERTICAL CYLINDER BELOW)

METAL

BLUE

Long and lean · *Concept art, Gibson Radsavanh* · The designs for Ninjago Tower incorporate both traditional architecture and modern ingenuity. The final build was one that only the medium of LEGO architecture could accomplish.

Amazing airlift • *Concept art, Kim Taylor* • Garmadon's flying squadron carries his volcano lair into NInjago City and place it on top of Ninjago Tower, which is to be his new lookout over his newly acquired minions.

Shark dock • *Animation development* • Computer-generated imagery shows how the tower top could accommodate Garmadon's Shark Mech.

Tiki party time • *Concept art, Kristen Anderson* • To celebrate his success, Garmadon throws a hastily coordinated tiki party with festive lighting and fun beverages on a platform of his new home.

TOWER-TOP PARTY

It's both a celebration of victory and a house-warming party when Lord Garmadon goes all out tiki-style. His army quickly leaps into party mode.

Ready to go • *Concept art (left), Gibson Radsavanh; storyboard art (below), John Puglisi and Natalie Wetzig* • At all stages of sketching, the concept of lights, drinks and music, was key to the party atmosphere.

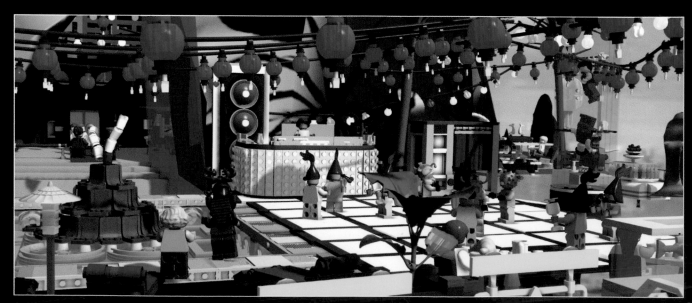

Party hearty • *Concept art, Kristen Anderson* • From lantern lights to conga lines and from banners to beverages served through a hose-tapped keg, the celebration on top of the Tower of Power is hard-earned and heartily appreciated by the Shark Army.

Cool dip • *Concept art, Kim Taylor* • A rooftop pool makes for a festive splash.

When I first saw this spread in art review, I have to admit that it made me hungry.

Kim Taylor, Production Designer

Smorgasbord • *Concept art, Kristen Anderson* • Conquering a city can work up a fierce appetite, so these plastic-but-palatable seafood treats are soon to be conquered as well.

Spin that vinyl (or plastic) • *Concept art (below left), Felicity Coonan* • This funky DJ spins the tunes to set the mood for minifigure dancing.

Two hats are better than one • *Concept art, Fiona Darwin* • Lord Garmadon shows a rare lighter side as he dons not one but two party hats, one hung from each of his evil helmet horns. Only the retention of his stern expression suggests he is not entirely in party mode.

THE JUNGLE

Beyond the live-action sequences in the film, the jungle setting is where the interplay between a natural-looking environment and the LEGO medium really comes into its own. Lush greenery abounds, with breathtaking vistas and rich flora that give the audience a sense of grandeur, while respecting the scale of LEGO minifigures in the scenes.

Going on a weapon hunt · *Concept art, Gibson Radsavanh, Fiona Darwin, Kim Taylor* · While on the path to find the Ultimate Ultimate Weapon to conquer Garmadon, the Secret Ninja Force must cross the "uncrossable jungle." On screen, the jungle has been given its impenetrable look through talented art direction, modelling, look development, special effects and matte painting of dense plantlife, deep ponds and misty waterfalls.

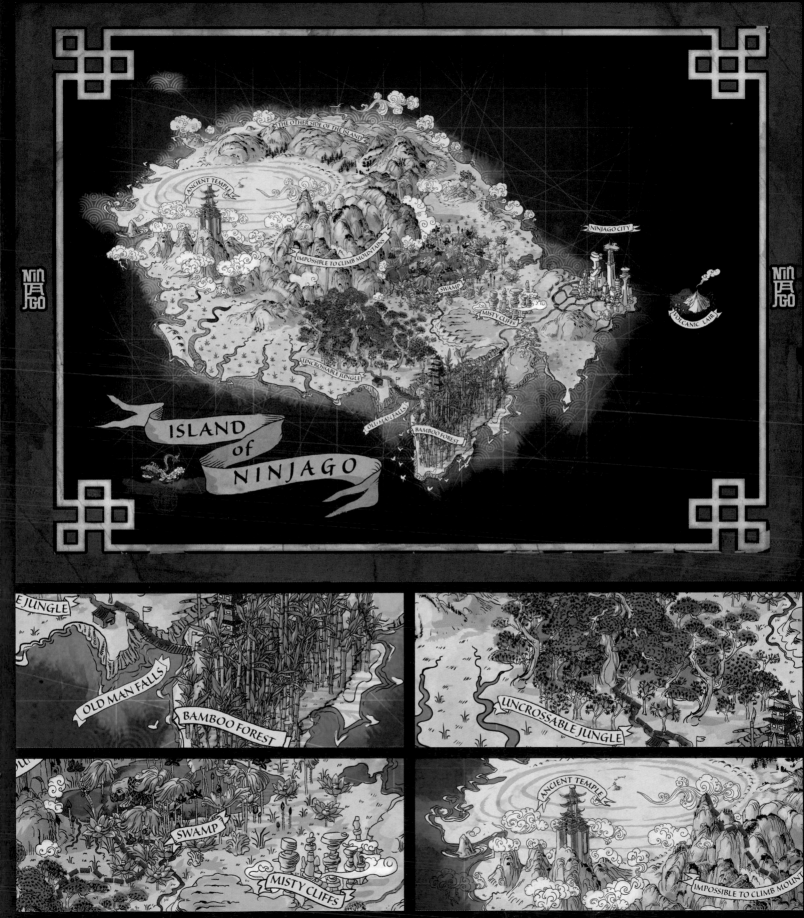

Follow the dotted line · *Concept art, Peter Commins and Felicity Coonan* · Vintage-style maps plot the path that the ninja follow, including a hike over the "impossible to climb mountain" and other challenges in the jungle.

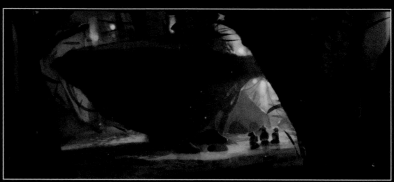

Black and white, yet green all over • *Concept art, Gibson Radsavanh* • The use of tonal key images helps to establish where light and dark areas in the jungle environment are, and where the audience's eye will be drawn to as they follow the ninja on their trek.

Swamp and shadow • *Concept art, Michael Halford, Kim Taylor* • The Secret Ninja Force must traverse a wide variety of natural obstacles, from swamps to ravines, all beautifully portrayed at minifigure scale.

A pass through the grass · *Colourscript image, Kim Taylor and Jessica Sommerville* · Crafting realistic-looking grass at a minifigure scale is a much bigger task than might be expected for such simple blades, as shown in these artworks.

Wet and wild · *Concept art, Kim Taylor, Ben Walker* · The creative efforts to portray streams, raindrops falling on a mossy bank and other water effects in a believable way have paid off with stunning results.

THE BRIDGE

During the course of the jungle expedition, Master Wu and the ninja encounter natural bridges formed by tree roots. There's also a long rope bridge that proves to be particularly challenging – it's a real cliffhanger moment, in fact!

Green with growth • *Concept art, Kim Taylor, Gibson Radsavanh, Noemie Cauvin* • Moss, dangling vines and intertwined roots make for beautifully lush – yet sometimes treacherous – walking paths. Intensive study of live plants helped the art direction team recreate them in minifigure scale with incredible accuracy.

"The bridge in the jungle is the setting for an epic battle between Garmadon and Wu!"

Simon Lucas, LEGO Senior Creative Director

The view from below • Concept art, *Michael Halford* • This shot of a tree root spanning the gorge shows just how far a fall from above would be.

Fearless leader falls • *Storyboard art (above left), John Puglisi; final render (above right)* • In a dramatic sequence, Master Wu is distracted by a butterfly and falls from a rope bridge, much to the shock and horror of the watching ninja.

Span-tastic • LEGO *model development, Luis F. E. Castaneda* • The rope bridge stretches across a deep gorge in the mountains, a length that must seem like miles in minifigure footsteps.

JUNGLE JOURNEY

The jungle trek is a lengthy one, requiring heavy lifting and overnight endurance on the part of the ninja force. These are tasks that the ninja aren't really prepared for, despite all their training. And without wise Master Wu to lead them, they must fend for themselves.

Slow but steady progress • *Storyboard art (top left), Bob Logan; colourscript image (bottom left), Kim Taylor; concept art (above), Ben Walker* • Once they have captured Garmadon, the ninja have an even heavier task at hand – carrying him in a cage through the jungle. These images not only show their progression, but also that of the painting process through various stages in the pre-animation pipeline.

THE TEMPLE

After a lengthy trek, the ninja arrive at their intended destination, an ancient temple. It's here they hope to discover the Ultimate Ultimate Weapon, but end up learning a little more history than they bargained for.

Snow-capped summit temple • *Concept art, Kim Taylor* • As if the jungle, mountains, rivers and rope bridges weren't enough of a challenge for the ninja's trek, in an early imagining they were to arrive at the base of the temple to find it a cold, icy and generally unwelcoming destination.

ABANDONED ABODE

It's not just an ancient temple after all: this site is the abandoned childhood home of brothers Lord Garmadon and Master Wu. Here, amongst the dust and spiders' webs, family history can be uncovered and a sought-after weapon found.

No welcome mat in sight • *Concept art, Matt Betteker (above), Gibson Radsavanh (below)* • Designers explored what the temple might look like in daytime and at night. This is the site that greets the ninja when the they approach this very daunting, old structure.

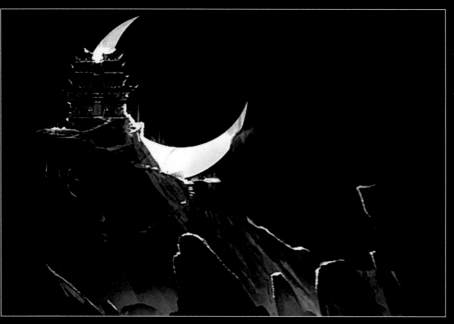

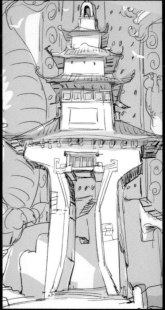

Tall and towering • *Concept art, Peter Commins* • Early sketches of the temple emphasise its lofty height and inaccessibility from the ground.

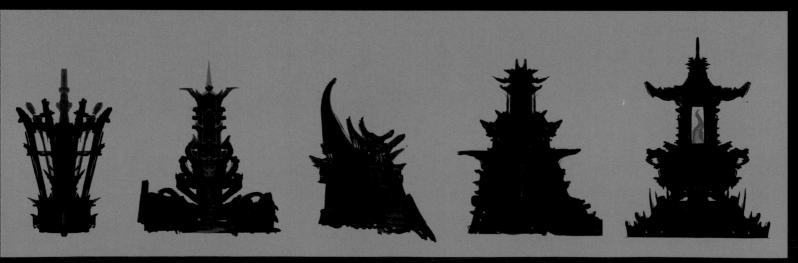

Top options • *Concept art, Gibson Radsavanh* • In order to create an interesting silhouette for the temple, special attention was paid to its roof design. Some options even suggest that this is where Garmadon found inspiration for the unusual pointed shape of his helmet.

Intriguing ingress · *Concept art, Kim Taylor, Gibson Radsavanh ·* The doorway into the temple echoes the strong red colour that Garmadon wears. Perhaps his choice in costume colour pays tribute to this element of his childhood home.

Dragon details · *Concept art, (above and far right), Noemie Cauvin and Peter Commins; modelling (right), David Whittaker and Jessica Sommerville ·* Highly detailed dragon pieces were crafted to serve as protectors and decorative elements outside the temple. This jade-green dragon was proposed to stand guard, in all of his regal glory, at the doorway.

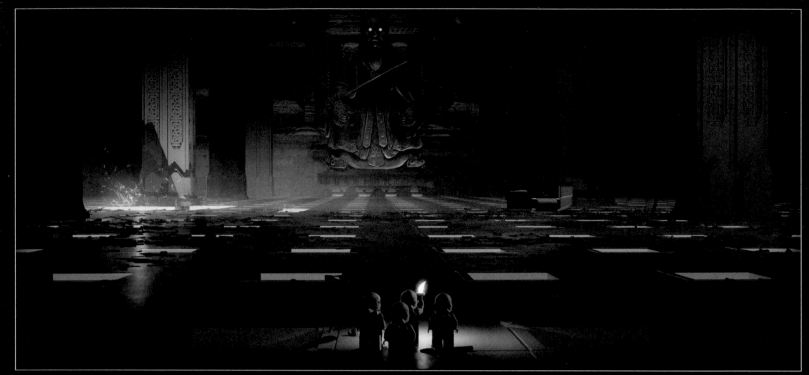

INSIDE THE TEMPLE

Once the ninja enter the temple, they are made to feel even more mini-than-minifigure size by the sheer expanse of the ancient space. Huge columns, grand halls, and many larger-than-life sculptures adorn every corner of every room they discover. Pillars cast long shadows across the floor.

Scary yet sanctified
• Concept art, Peter Commins, Gibson Radsavanh • Although the temple is now filled with litter and dust, the space still seems eerily sacred in the soft glow of candlelight.

Home is where the history is • *Storyboard art (left), Januel Mercado; concept art (right), Gibson Radsavanh* • Garmadon and the ninja survey the space in which Wu and his brother once enjoyed each other's company, long before they ended up on opposing sides.

Father-son showdown • *Concept art, Dudley Birch* • The family tradition of fighting amongst themselves continues in the next generation in this image as Lloyd and his father face off with one another. This is, after all, the place where it all started between the men of the Garmadon family.

Model homes • LEGO *model development, Michael Svane Knap* • A LEGO "boost session" was the occasion for constructing these temple models. Many bricks were laid as the designer experimented with different entrances and guards for the front door.

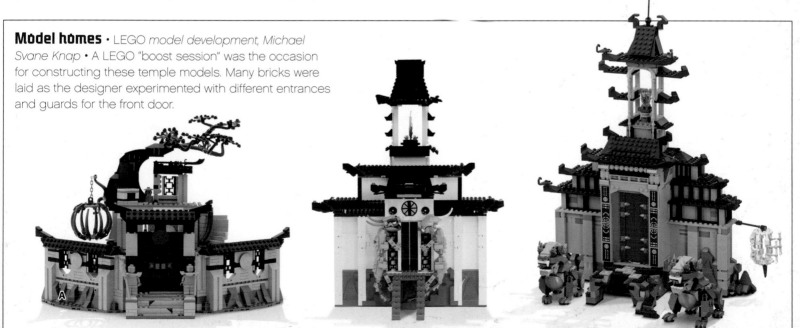

GENERALS' LAIR

Lord Garmadon may have used the "out of sight, out of mind" approach with his generals, but once fired out of his volcano lair, where do they really go? Apparently the trajectory of the volcano's blast has landed them in the heart of the jungle. From this deep, dark location they have rallied and planned revenge for their unceremonious dismissals.

Follow the light • *Concept art, Peter Commins* • The ninja and the audience are both drawn to the light, wondering what could be hidden in the middle of the jungle.

We shall rebuild • *Colourscript image, Kim Taylor* • The fired generals have gathered themselves and set up their own fort, here pictured in true classic LEGO block form.

Sandy approach • *Render, Jessica Sommerville* • A rough computer-generated render, known as a "stand-in-set," is used for the generals' lair whilst the final one is being built.

> **"**I really loved the idea of dried-up canals for the city of lost generals. I wanted to give the generals the high ground so that anyone arriving would feel vulnerable and at their mercy.**"**
>
> **Kim Taylor, Production Designer**

Walled off · *Concept art, Kim Taylor* · A mighty fortress has been built by the fired generals, a testament to how they really do not want to be caught off-guard a second time.

Eight-legged welcome · *Concept art, Michael Halford* · An octopus banner flies high above the generals' lair, with posts constructed from LEGO skeleton pieces.

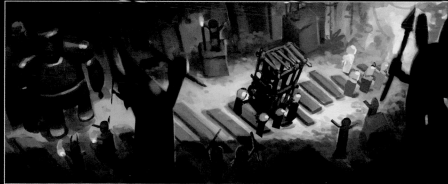

Community among the excommunicated · *Concept art, Gibson Radsavanh* · Inside their formidable fortress, the guards have created a surprisingly pleasant environment in which their egos can heal. The tentative approach of the ninja is shown in simple, coloured shapes.

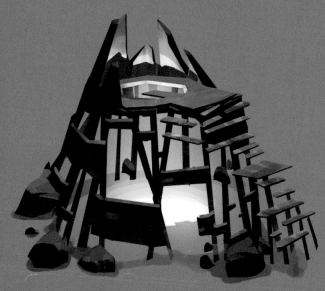

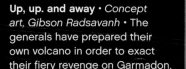

Up, up. and away · *Concept art, Gibson Radsavanh* · The generals have prepared their own volcano in order to exact their fiery revenge on Garmadon.

PLACES THAT NEVER WERE

While many potential storylines were explored in the making of THE LEGO NINJAGO MOVIE, many potential locations were designed. Here are a few interesting sites that are found only on the deserted story paths for the film and not in the final cut.

Green hills, green tea • *Concept art, Peter Commins (above), Dudley Birch (left)* • To follow the concept that *Destiny's Bounty* is a tea barge – not a secret ninja training facility – there was once a storyline that explored the place where tea was cultivated under the guidance of Wu. Reminiscent of rice paddies and karsts, the tea plantation was imagined as a lush, pleasant environment.

"Often we explore locations and characters that are never seen in the movie but are part of the filmmaking process."

Kristen Murtha, Associate Producer

Tea plantation • *Concept art, Kim Taylor and Grant Freckelton* • This rural setting lent itself to more traditional transport methods, such as horses, than the mechs found in Ninjago City.

Ancient village · *Concept art, Takumer Homma* · Citizens gather in the town centre to discuss how to deal with the threat of a "Big Snake" (known as the Great Devourer) in a former version of the story.

Mongoose vs Snake · *Concept art, Kim Taylor and Takumer Homma (above), Peter Commins (right)* · Constructing a big mongoose to battle the Great Devourer was the citizens' answer to the reptilian threat. In the final film, the mongoose can be seen as a statue in Ninjago City, a tribute to a story that never was.

Inside out · *Concept art, Kim Taylor* · "The belly of the beast" is a fire-filled place that two of the ninja explored after being swallowed by the big snake.

CHARACTERS

LLOYD GARMADON

Lloyd hasn't had it easy growing up as the paternally abandoned yet publicly recognised son of evil Lord Garmadon. However, he has learned to redirect that negativity into positive work as a member of the Secret Ninja Force, protecting Ninjago City from attack.

Big daddy issues • *Storyboard art, Maggie Kang* • Poor Lloyd spends a lot of time in big open spaces trying to sort out his monumental parental problems.

Deep dark thoughts • *Concept art, Donald Walker* • These line drawings show the downtrodden effects that being the son of an evil warlord could have on a young man.

Youthful vigor • *Concept art, Lianne Hughes* • The youngest of the ninja, Lloyd has perhaps the most innocent facial expressions of the team.

Hoodwinked • *Concept art, Fiona Darwin (above), Tim Pyman (far left), Gibson Radsavanh (left)* • Perhaps in an effort to keep a low profile due to his infamous father, Lloyd wears a hood. This required a great deal of design work to capture an appealing shape while allowing a clear view of his face. Existing LEGO® hoods, such as one worn by Little Red Riding Hood, were trialled before a new piece was decided on.

Blonde and bold • *Concept art, Felicity Coonan (top); LEGO model development, Gibson Radsavanh, Paul M. Wood, Stewart Whitehead* • As with all the ninja, hair shape is key to establishing a unique silhouette. Lloyd's white-blonde shag cut went through a variety of styles before choosing the perfect LEGO wig piece, also seen poking out beneath his hood.

THE GREEN NINJA

Green Ninja Lloyd leads the Secret Ninja Force with great energy and charisma. Even though he wrestles with his past and his complicated family, Lloyd knows that when he is in ninja mode he must always do what is best for the citizens of Ninjago City.

Action pose • *Concept art, Kim Taylor* • Green Ninja Lloyd embodies the spirit of his Energy powers, leaping into explosive action.

Being seen in green • *Concept art, Nadia Attlee, Kim Taylor, Fiona Darwin* • The Green Ninja's costume development went through many shades of green and different amounts of gold detailing.

Emblematic energy • *Graphic art, Felicity Coonan* • This round emblem represents all six ninja united in a circle, but personalised for each individual. The design is also reminiscent in style of an atomic energy symbol.

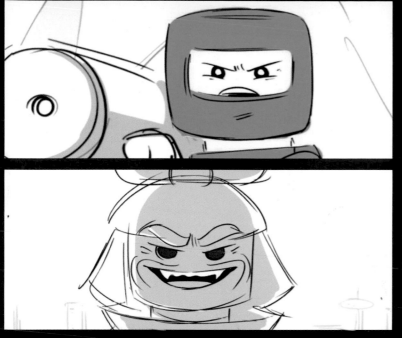

Father vs son • *Storyboard art, Maggie Kang; concept art, Michael Halford (top right)* • Key dramatic moments in the film come from the scenes between Lloyd and Lord Garmadon. These storyboards reveal a depth of emotion, played out by the LEGO minifigure characters, that viewers can empathise with.

" I admire Lloyd's spirit in the face of adversity. **"**

Matt Everitt, Animation Director

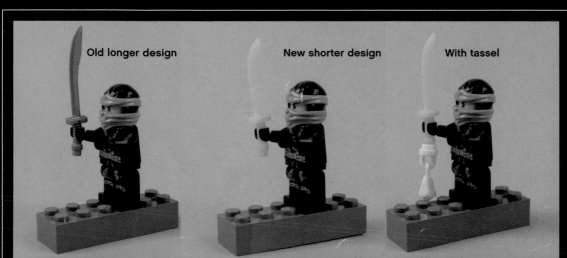

Old longer design   New shorter design   With tassel

Ways of weaponry • LEGO *model development, Jakob Rune Nielsen* • The Green Ninja carries a serious sword. The final version was found on the cutting edge of cool design and toy safety, after considering options with and without the ornamental tassel.

NYA

Nya is a go-with-the-flow kind of gal, focused and strong but ready to shift with the tide of whatever situation she's immersed in. Nya knows how to hold her own, whether she's in the realm of high school or in ninja combat action.

Read my lips •
Concept art, Carey Yost • With Nya being the only female ninja, the designers enjoyed giving her strong and spirited expressions.

The hair up there · LEGO *model development, Nicholas Timothy Whitmore* · Nya's hair went through many different styles before the perfect shape was found to give both a clear silhouette and allow her facial expressions to be read. Designers experimented along the way with adding hair accessories, including a hair band.

> "I can really relate to this strong girl – to her boldness, toughness and strength – holding her own."

Maryann Garger, Producer

Fashion frenzy · *Concept art, Nadia Attlee, Felicity Coonan, Fiona Darwin* · From studded leather to buttoned wool, and from solid colors and bowties to stripes and pendants, Nya's casual and school-uniform considerations spanned several hairstyles and closets worth of options.

THE SILVER NINJA

When in ninja mode, Nya knows how to strike the right pose while striking her foes. With her power coming from the element of water, the Silver Ninja is a true force of nature and a spear-wielding warrior.

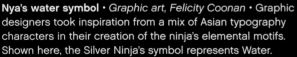

Nya's water symbol · *Graphic art, Felicity Coonan* · Graphic designers took inspiration from a mix of Asian typography characters in their creation of the ninja's elemental motifs. Shown here, the Silver Ninja's symbol represents Water.

Gray is the new black · *Concept art, Tim Pyman (left), Kim Taylor (right)* · Concept artists explored many variations in armour for the Silver Ninja, including different accessories and motifs.

Standing strong • *Concept art, Dudley Birch* • The Silver Ninja embodies an undercurrent of power that makes her an honourable ninja.

Shielded by her skirt • LEGO *model development, Nina Buch Rasmussen* • The design team created a new, fabric LEGO element for the Silver Ninja's skirt – a functional, protective, wraparound piece.

"We had to find a line between rough'n'tough and feminine that wasn't thwarted by the base shape of the minifigure itself."

Fiona Darwin, Concept Artist

COLE

Cole is almost too cool for school, but he does actually attend class when he's not busy being a secret ninja. He exudes confidence in a street-smart DJ-rocker way, headphones in place as much as possible, but with a touch of gratuitous selfie moments thrown in just for fun.

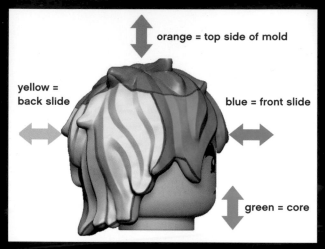

Locks that rock • *Design, Felicity Coonan; LEGO model development, Stew Whitehead* • Cole's hairstyle required many layers of sculpting to find the right silhouette. The result was captured in a brand-new LEGO brick mould.

orange = top side of mold

yellow = back slide

blue = front slide

green = core

Brows abound • *Concept art, Carey Yost (top), Lianne Hughes (bottom)* • The progression of expression from rough pencil sketch to LEGO design draft maintains Cole's strong personality.

> **"**Cole is the cool kid… his school/civvie outfit needed to hint at this so we asked the question "what would he listen to?" The answer was obvious – AC/DC! – a bit old school, hard rock and rebellious.**"**
>
> **Felicity Coonan, Art Director**

Hard rock clothing • *Concept art, Felicity Coonan, Nadia Attlee* • Cole's connection to rock is twofold – one in musical interest, and two in his love of outdoor climbing. Designers had fun crossing earth-bound sayings into rock'n'roll styled shirts, and also into Ninjago Language symbols.

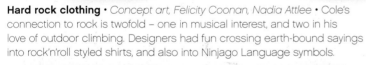

THE STUDS

DIRT ROCKS

SEISMIC

QUAKE

THE BLACK NINJA

Grounded Cole, aka the Black Ninja, exhibits unwavering strength, focus and impressive coolness in even the most heated moments of battle. In fact, the words "battle time" are like music to his ears.

Grounded guy • *Concept art, Dudley Birch* • Confident Cole harnesses the mighty power that lies beneath the Earth.

To bun or not to bun • *Concept art, Tim Pyman, Felicity Coonan, Fiona Darwin* • Designers made the task of styling Cole's hair a top priority, with a neat man-bun as part of their exploration.

Triple style for double threat • *Concept art, Fiona Darwin* • From high-school student to full-on fighter, Cole's costume change maintains his level of cool confidence with simple palette tones.

Down to earth • *Graphic art, Felicity Coonan* • Cole's elemental power comes from the Earth and gives him solid fighting strength, as symbolised with this emblem.

Pounding down • *Concept art, Nadia Attlee, Fiona Darwin* • The Earth Ninja's weapon of choice went through its own evolution. This lineup hammers home the thoughtful design process undertaken for each minifigure, ending with his final ninja look.

KAI

Kai is the hot-headed, high-energy member of the Secret Ninja Force. It's almost as if he can't contain himself at times, from his zippy walk to his fast-paced talk. In all things, Kai's minifigure form reflects the big, bold body language and personality of his character.

Expressions to the extreme • *Concept art, Lianna Hughes* • With so much energy, Kai can push his facial features into really expressive poses.

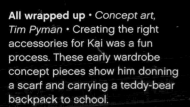

All wrapped up • *Concept art, Tim Pyman* • Creating the right accessories for Kai was a fun process. These early wardrobe concept pieces show him donning a scarf and carrying a teddy-bear backpack to school.

Racer boy, but not to the finish • *Concept art, Gibson Radsavanh, Tim Pyman* • Early renditions of Kai's costume resembled a racing-car driver's suit. This look made sense for a speedy teenager, but was not ideal for an undercover ninja.

Swooptastic style
• *Design, Felicity Coonan* •
Different options for Kai's
hairstyle were tried out.
Each variation subtly
different, they all seem to
resemble a flame-like
silhouette to visually cue his
hot-headed nature and his
Fire elemental symbol.

"Kai is so likeable:
he's funny and awkward,
like that friend who can
always get away with
saying the wrong thing
in such an innocent
way because he's
so endearing."

Fiona Chilton, Associate Producer

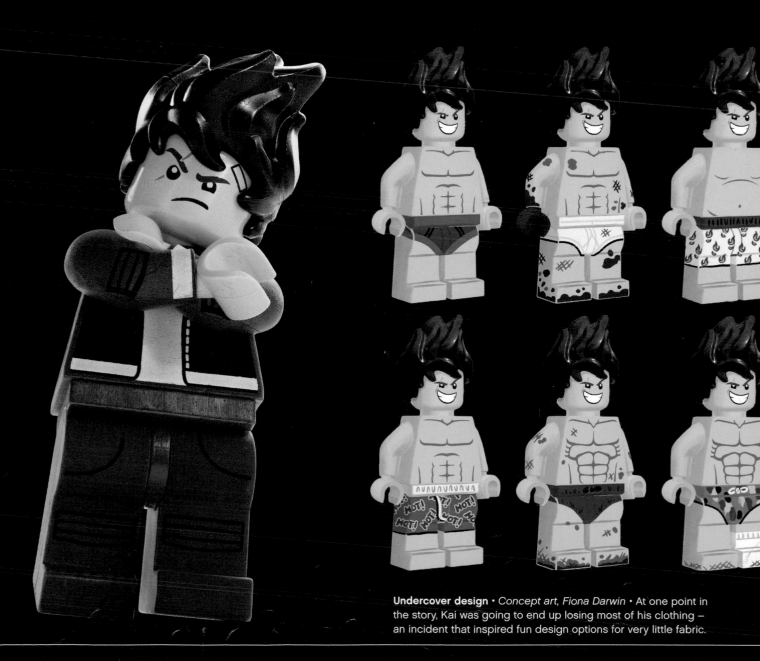

Undercover design • *Concept art, Fiona Darwin* • At one point in
the story, Kai was going to end up losing most of his clothing –
an incident that inspired fun design options for very little fabric.

THE RED NINJA

Red Ninja Kai burns up any battle scene with his fierce, flaming energy. Mastering the katanas as his weapon of choice, the Red Ninja enters every fight in a blaze of double-handed glory.

Fiery fighter • *Graphic art, Felicity Coonan* • The Red Ninja's elemental power is that of Fire. The graphic, red-and-black representation of this symbol morphed through various phases of development.

Fighting fantastic in plastic • *Hood design, Kim Taylor, Simon Whiteley, Pierre Salazar, Niels Milan Pedersen, Stewart Whitehead* • New moulds were developed by the LEGO Group for the ninja hoods worn by all members of the Secret Ninja Force. The hoods innovatively feature a headband knotted at the back. When ready to roll, Kai's katana swords slot into an already existing LEGO piece.

WARNING: SUPER HOT

High temperature slogan • *Graphic art* • The Red Ninja comes with his own "super hot" warning sign.

Dragons and other details
• *Concept art, Tim Pyman* •
The design of the Red Ninja's robe and armour worked through various red-hot sashes and dragon motifs before the final look was decided.

Red and ready • *Final render* • Springing into action, the Red Ninja is a fast and fired-up part of the team.

ZANE

Affectionately known as a robot-boy, Zane is a
Nindroid who is also the president (and only
member) of the high school audiovisual club.
Due to his mechanical capabilities, he is also the
equipment for that AV club, projecting movies
from his eye with his own built-in hipster filter.

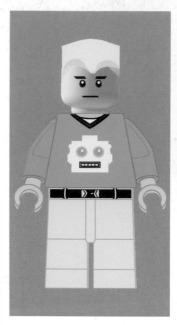

Dressed in digital • *Concept art, Nadia Attlee* • Zane's wardrobe
reflects his robotic background and incorporates fun computer-
game style designs.

In control • *Final render* • Part technology himself,
Zane is the go-to guy for all things electronic.

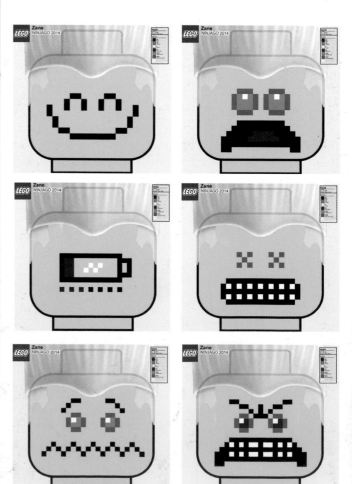

8-bit in 6 expressions • *Concept art, Charles Santoso* • Character
designers had fun with the fact that Zane is part robot, expressing
his emotions in pixelated 8-bit style.

> **"**Zane's robotic nature allows the animators to really have fun with the way that he interacts with the world and how he relates to people around him.**"**
>
> **Matt Everitt, Animation Director**

Cut short · *Concept art, Felicity Coonan* · Unlike most of his high-school ninja pals, Zane's hair designs were all styled much tighter to his head, with the final choice a sharply chopped "flat top" style.

Technology on demand · *Concept art, Gibson Radsavanh* · Zane's talents make him ready to roll, whether it's for ninja duty or projector duty, such as playing a video about Lord Garmadon to the class.

THE WHITE NINJA

The White Ninja is calm, cool and calculating, thanks in part to his robotic side. Some might think Zane's lack of emotions make him less human, but he believes it leaves him freer to be more ninja.

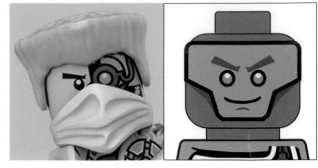

Two-faced • *Existing LEGO® NINJAGO™ models* • Representing Zane's half-human, half-robot mix was a particular challenge for the designers. Inspired by existing Zane minifigures, his ninja expression was tried out in machine-grey before moving back to classic LEGO yellow.

Ice ice baby • *Graphic art, Felicity Coonan* • The elemental power of the White Ninja is Ice, as crystallised in these symbolic graphic designs.

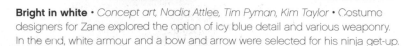

Bright in white • *Concept art, Nadia Attlee, Tim Pyman, Kim Taylor* • Costume designers for Zane explored the option of icy blue detail and various weaponry. In the end, white armour and a bow and arrow were selected for his ninja get-up.

Arrowed and ready • *Concept art, Michael Halford* • Zane uses his high-tech brain to shoot his high-powered arrows with startling accuracy.

The face behind the face • *Concept art, Fiona Darwin* • To know the White Ninja is to know what he looks like under his classic LEGO façade. Designers considered numerous inner workings before selecting the chosen display.

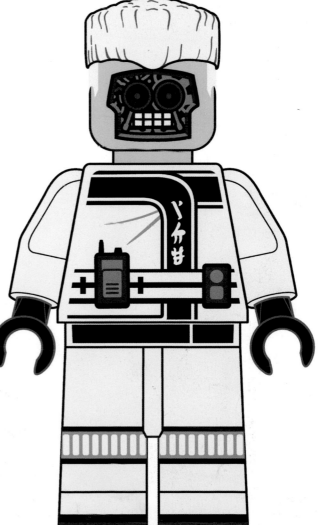

JAY

Young Jay exhibits fun and funny neuroses that make his character all the more entertaining. Harbouring a crush on fellow ninja Nya, Jay is eager to please, eager for fans, and eager to look good in his fine orange scarf and as the Blue Ninja.

Smiles and such • *Concept art, Lianne Hughes* • Jay goes through a range of emotions on a daily basis, so designers had fun detailing his confusion, anxiety and cheer.

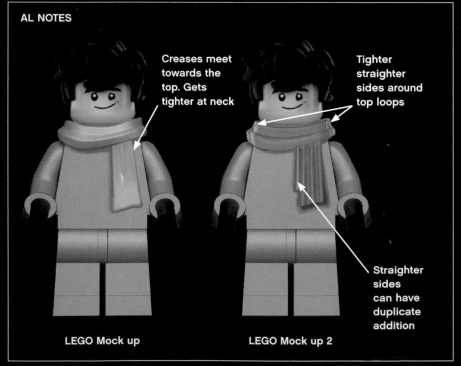

AL NOTES

Creases meet towards the top. Gets tighter at neck

Tighter straighter sides around top loops

Straighter sides can have duplicate addition

LEGO Mock up

LEGO Mock up 2

Fab fake fabric • *Design, Tim Pyman, Pierre Salazar, Carsten Lind* • Considering how challenging it is to make something cast in hard plastic look like fabric, the costume design team focused their attention when working on Jay's scarf. Designers also worked in jacket details to allude to Jay's "Lighning Ninja" alter ego.

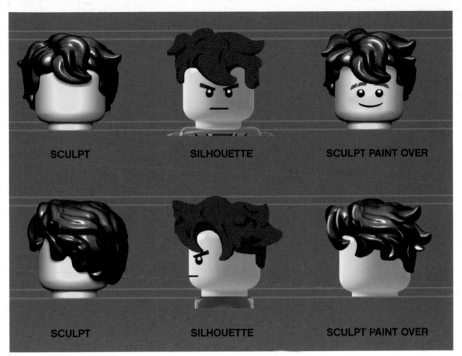

Shocking style · *Concept art, Felicity Coonan, Stewart Whitehead* · The concept for Jay's tousled hair grew from the idea that he may have been struck by lightning at some point in his life, causing curls. Jay draws his elemental power from Lightning when in ninja mode.

Meet Mom and Dad · *Design, Fiona Darwin, Nadia Attlee, Lars Roersen Nielsen* · Ed and Edna, Jay's beloved adoptive and seashell-collecting parents, make a short-but-sweet appearance in THE LEGO® NINJAGO® MOVIE™. They will finally be made into physical minifigure existence with the release of this film.

THE BLUE NINJA

In his secret double life as the Blue Ninja, Jay battles alongside his teammates while maintaining a good sense of humour in even the most challenging moments.

Suited and booted for the sky • *Concept art, Tim Pyman •* An early option for Jay, who flies a Lightning Jet mech, saw him wearing pilot's gear over the top of his ninja outfit as he took to the skies.

True lightning-blue • *Exisiting LEGO NINJAGO minifigures •* In the LEGO NINJAGO television series, the Blue Ninja has worn many different suits of armour and had very different hair!

New robes, new weapons ·
Design, Nadia Attlee, Fiona Darwin · A notable number of armour and weapon variations were considered for the Blue Ninja including, at one point, a conical hat. His final model wields a flail.

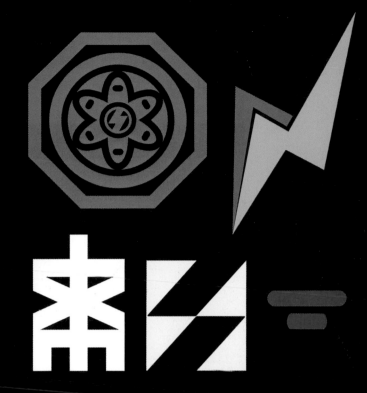

Electrical element · *Graphic art, Felicity Coonan* · The Blue Ninja is driven by the elemental power of Lightning, zapped into graphic form in these symbol designs.

Lightning-fast · *Concept art, Dudley Birch* · The Blue Ninja's elemental power shines through when he moves with lightning speed above Ninjago City.

SECRET NINJA FORCE

The team of six consider themselves "so ninja" with all their
martial arts and mech-manoeuvring skills. However, Master
Wu tries to teach them that there are greater factors at work.

Tornado of Creation • *Concept art, Yannick Tan (left), Ben Walker (top right), Dudley Birch (middle and bottom right)* • The Secret Ninja Force finds success in their physical combat, but they can do even greater, colourful and more constructive things if they tap into their inner balance.

MASTER WU

Master Wu is the old-school mentor to a very new-school team of ninja. He seeks to instil the power of Spinjitzu into the young fighters by teaching them about the powers they have within themselves. He encourages them not to rely on new-fangled machines.

Minifigure minisketch • *Concept art, Charlie Bean* • An early rendition of Master Wu captured the essence of his small-village costume styling. This straw hat was later returned to for Lord Garmadon's jungle outfit, whereas brother Wu ended up wearing a more traditional conical design.

Clearly kung-fu • *Concept art, Tim Pyman, Felicity Coonan (top), Fiona Darwin (right)* • Early designs for Wu's costume show heavy influence from traditional kung-fu.

"Master Wu needed more ageing and dirt to suggest a minifigure that has been around for many years. This meant more detailing than the average character – custom-painted damage, dirt... plus frayed edging on the woven cloth of his robe."

JP LeBlanc, Look Development Supervisor

Robe of respect • *Concept art, Fiona Darwin, Dudley Birch* • Once Wu's minifigure model was chosen, robe details were woven into the design process before being painted on both fabric and plastic.

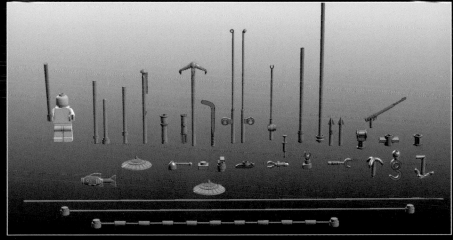

Catching anything that swims • *Concept art, Kristen Anderson* • The line-up of fishing gear developed for Master Wu is extensive and extremely handy given how much time he spends on the water in *Destiny's Bounty*.

More than meets the eye, or the ear • *Concept art, Fiona Darwin* • Wu's staff doubles as a musical instrument and would probably be useful in hand-to-hand combat if needed.

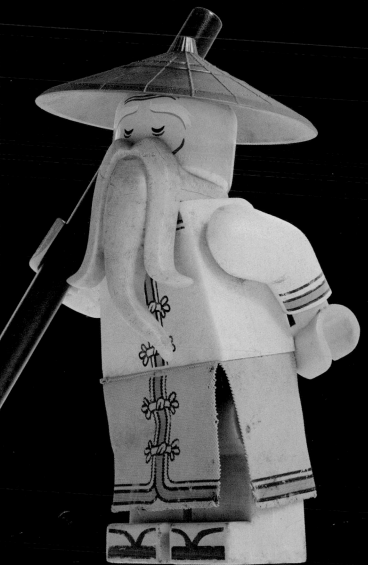

Action when required • *Concept art, Kim Taylor* • This early, beardless, concept art shows that Master Wu can unleash powerful energy when the fight requires more than just a calm sage.

Lost his hat but not his cool • *Concept art, Ben Walker* • Master Wu is shown in a rare uncapped moment, deep in the jungle.

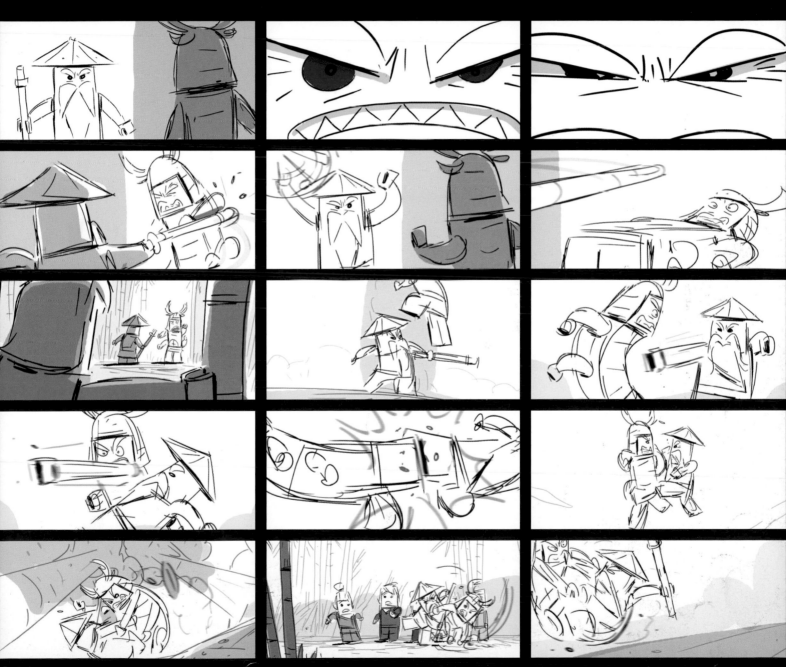

Brother vs brother • *Storyboard art, John Puglisi* • Intricate fight moves bust out between Wu and Garmadon, with fighting techniques choreographed by none other than Jackie Chan himself, and his team.

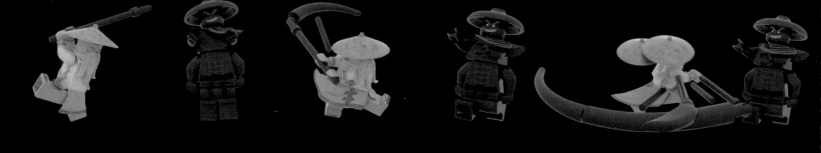

The light and dark side of brotherhood • *Animation development* •
Wu and his sibling Garmadon may have been built from the same
bricks, but they each turned out very differently. The two are
locked into opposite sides of the battle for Ninjago City and have
different opinions on how to raise Lloyd – Wu's nephew and
Garmadon's son.

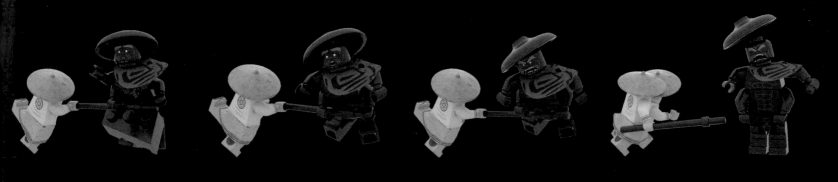

Blow by blow · *Animation development* · Master Wu produces unexpectedly swift martial arts moves for an aged guy. Having Jackie Chan and his stunt crew in Beijing choreograph the fight scenes certainly gives Wu a leg up (and kicking) in combat.

YOUNG SIBLINGS

It's hard to believe that Master Wu and Lord Garmadon are brothers, since they are far from being brothers-in-arms. If only the evil snake had not bitten Garmadon and turned him bad, who knows what life in Ninjago City would be like without such strong sibling rivalry?

Turning back time • *Concept art, Tim Pyman* • *Concept artists portrayed the brothers in their youth in numerous costume pairings but with consistently recognisable facial expressions.*

Wig-tastic Wu · *Concept art, Pierre Salazar* · A sculpt turnaround of Wu's youthful hairstyle is interestingly reminiscent of a wise old sage, even at a young age.

Young Wu, young do · *Concept art, Tim Pyman* · The fringe, headband and facial hair may have varied, but the man-bun was well planted on the young Wu, with a darker hair colouring.

SENSEI WU & GARMADON LINE UP
"THEN & NOW"

THIS BLUE SHOULD EXIST AS A DECAL COLOUR
BUT ISN'T PART OF THE LEGO PLASTIC COLOUR RANGE
(I.E. WE CAN'T MOLD ANYTHING IN THIS COLOUR)

CLOSEST OFFICIAL
LEGO COLOURS

How do you blue? · *Concept art, Tim Pyman* · During costume development for Garmadon and Wu, the challenge of working within the LEGO colour palette range required thoughtful design considerations.

LORD GARMADON

Garmadon is an evil warlord who wants nothing more than to defeat Ninjago City and rule it with his heavy (multiple) handed ways. He is so self-centred that he has no idea that he makes his son Lloyd's life a torment. In fact, he hasn't even learnt how to pronounce Lloyd's name correctly.

2b. (WITH ROBE)

Elegant yet evil · *Graphic art, Felicity Coonan* · No matter how classy Garmadon's symbol may look, looks can be deceiving – that beauty actually represents his villainous nature. Early options for his symbol included "E" for "evil" and "T" for "tyrant."

Breaking new ground · *Concept art, Tim Pyman* · This early sketch of four-armed, robed Lord Garmadon captured the essence of the villain. Approximately 150 designs followed, before designers returned to a look very similar to this.

The arms have it · *Concept art, Kim Taylor* · Working through poses for Garmadon is twice as challenging, yet twice as fun, for animation artists, due to Garmadon's extra limbs.

"Garmadon is a bad guy to the core… he's always true to who he is: even when he's trying to be sincere, everything he says comes out filtered through his evil nature and the results are always hilarious. Garmadon is a villain you can't help but love."

Maggie Kang, Head of Story

A face only a mother could love… maybe • *Concept art, Lianne Hughes* • Lord Garmadon's recognisably intimidating face did not change much from his look in the TV series. But it required much exploration to create a range of expressions bad and bold enough for the big screen.

NINJAGO CITY'S MOST WANTED

As if Lord Garmadon's glaring red eyes are not intimidating enough, this bad guy also sports a threatening-looking helmet and wields a serious weapon… and in his downtime, patterned pyjamas.

6 cm
5.5
5 cm
4.5
4 cm
3.5
3 cm

94277715

NINJAGO CITY
WORST BAD GUY
GARMADON

WANTED
FOR CHAOS AND DESTRUCTION

Be on the lookout! • *Concept art, Felicity Coonan* • Designed for the "worst guy ever" flashback sequence, this image of Garmadon is inspired by old-time criminal posters.

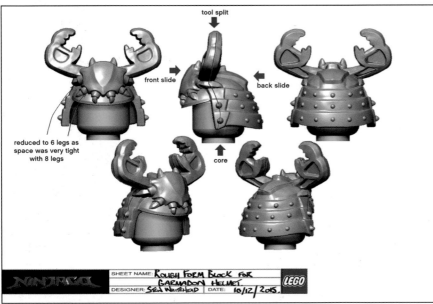

tool split

front slide

back slide

reduced to 6 legs as space was very tight with 8 legs

core

| SHEET NAME: ROUGH FORM BLOCK FOR GARMADON HELMET | LEGO |
| DESIGNER: STEW WHITEHEAD | DATE: 10/12/2015. |

Humor or heathen • *Concept art, Gibson Radsavanh, Fiona Darwin; LEGO model development, Stewart Whitehead* • Helmet design exploration ranged from funny options such as antlers and sharks, all the way through to diabolical double horns. The final result was frightening yet approachable, and required a whole new mould piece.

Bad from head to toe • LEGO *model development, Nina Buch Rasmussen, Stewart Whitehead* • To achieve Garmadon's intimidating height, LEGO designers worked on ways for his chestplate to accomodate both extra arms and prop his head up higher than on a normal minifigure. His fabric cloak then drapes over his long body piece. All this combines to create a menacing minifigure who casts a long shadow over Ninjago City!

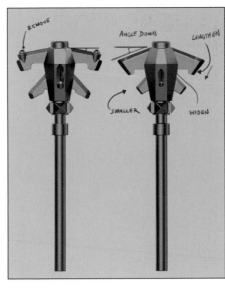

Putting a fine point on it · Concept art, *Gibson Radsavanh; development work, Luis F. E. Castaneda, Esa Petteri Nousiainen* · A tough guy such as Garmadon needs a tough weapon. His final staff was inspired by shapes that LEGO designers had put into Garmadon's mech.

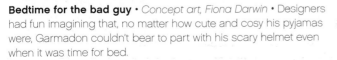

Bedtime for the bad guy · *Concept art, Fiona Darwin* · Designers had fun imagining that, no matter how cute and cosy his pyjamas were, Garmadon couldn't bear to part with his scary helmet even when it was time for bed.

KOKO

Koko is an awesome mother to Lloyd. She is hard-working and ready to whip up a batch of pancakes or positive attitude, whichever will help when Lloyd's feeling down about his stigmatised social status or paternal lineage. As caring as she is, it's a wonder that Koko doesn't realise Lloyd has a secret life. Perhaps she is just too busy with her own secret life?

The ideal mum • *Concept art, Fiona Darwin* • Character designers worked through various hairstyles, hair colours and wardrobe choices to create the perfect modern-day Koko.

> "Koko is a strong mom who is actually stronger than you might think at first glance."
>
> **Dan Lin, Producer**

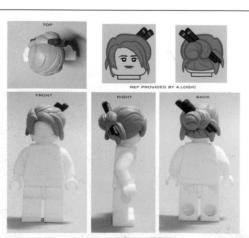

Ready to eat at the drop of a hairpin • *Design, Fiona Darwin; LEGO model development, Stewart Whitehead* • The challenge of moulding the chopsticks in Koko's hair into a LEGO piece was truly hair-raising. The final result was the creation of an entirely new LEGO wig piece.

Quick-change cut •
Final render • If only everyone could change their hairstyle as quickly as Koko is able to! Her fast moves in the apartment leave even Lloyd with a raised eyebrow or two.

Ancient history •
Final renders • Koko and Lord Garmadon might share a son, but they no longer see eye-to-eye. Koko's normally calm persona is replaced by motherly rage when it transpires that her former partner is responsible for Lloyd vanishing.

KOKO'S FLASHBACK

Just how did Lloyd's parents meet, you ask? And Lloyd wonders, too. Lloyd's mother, Koko, answers that very question with a look back into the past to where it all supposedly began.

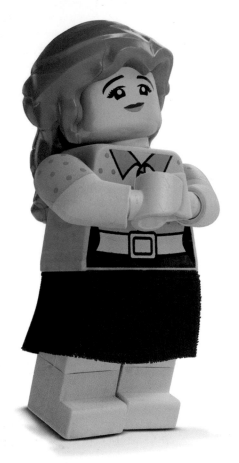

Seventies style • *Concept art, Fiona Darwin* • In her early career, Koko claims she worked in an office and wore fashionable frocks complete with groovy designs, jumpers, and trouser suits. On her wedding day, she was radiant in her classically conservative wedding gown – purely innocent of what was to come after marrying Garmadon.

Budding romance at the office • *Storyboard art, Bob Logan; final frames* • "I was in mergers, he was in hostile takeovers" is what Koko explains to Lloyd in her version of events, as shown in these story panels.

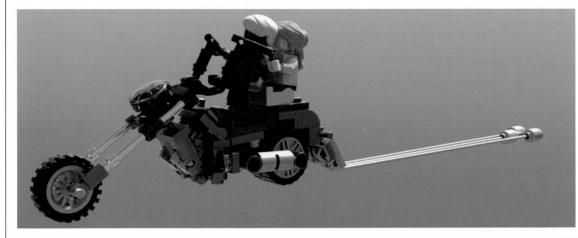

Easy riders · *Concept art, Jessica Sommerville* · Ahh, to be young and in love, and cruising into the sunset on a groovy chopper. This is the way Koko remembers the early days of her romance with Garmadon, not unlike a 1970s motorcycle movie. Who wouldn't fall for someone with such impressive exhaust pipes on his bike? Cans trail behind beneath a "just hitched" sign, all represented in LEGO parts, to represent their newlywed status.

> "Garmadon and Koko's history was the key to the whole thing. The movie is built around a father/son journey, but it's really the story of a family."

Paul Fisher, Writer/Director

Garm in office garb · *Concept art, Fiona Darwin* · Wide ties, wild prints and leisure-suit luxury made up Garmadon's past style sense – plus a smooth comb-over. It's no wonder Koko fell for this fashion plate!

LADY IRON DRAGON

In a surprise twist, it turns out this awesome mum is also an awesome warrior! Lady Iron Dragon is the secret alternative identity of Koko, which may also explain Lloyd's success as a ninja – it runs in the family!

Armoured and dangerous • *Concept art, Fiona Darwin* • The wardrobe ideas, especially the helmet options, for Lady Iron Dragon varied greatly during the design process, but all were both impressive and intimidating.

Sealed with a kiss • *Storyboard art, Bob Logan; concept art, Fiona Darwin (bottom right)* • "Fight first, then fall into each others' arms" is how Garmadon recalls the good old days with his Lady Iron Dragon. This storyboard reveals the truth behind how Koko and Garmadon met, in stark contrast with the version Koko gives Lloyd.

Bowed and beautiful • LEGO *model development, Esa Petteri Nousiainen* • Arrows and a crossbow are in Lady Iron Dragon's bag of tricks, ready to be drawn and fired at a moment's notice. Her quiver of arrows is affixed to her armour pieces and worn with her unique helmet, beneath which her hair piece is styled to fit but not look too neat.

"Koko is actually something of a wild child, but she chose to settle down for the sake of her son."

Paul Fisher, Writer/Director

SHARK ARMY

Garmadon's henchmen are a real bunch of waterfront thugs. They've rejected the daily grind of being fishermen and dockworkers in favour of working for an evil leader. Not the brightest fish in the shoal, these guys are looking to get the job done in the easiest, least verbal, and most physical way – while dressed as scary sea-themed creatures.

An army of ideas • *Concept art, Peter Commins, Mark Sexton, Tim Pyman* • Designers dived deep in order to come up with fun yet frightening battle garb for Garmadon's army. Eels, an octopus, crawfish, squid, crabs and even ghostly looking pirates lined the ranks in the development phase.

"The Shark Army thugs mostly act with relative uninspired stupidity and, though they love a good fight, only the fear of Garmadon will keep them in line when they appear to be losing."

Kim Taylor, Production Designer

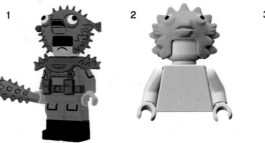

Spiky sculpting · LEGO *model development, Jakob Rune Nielsen* · The puffer fish is certainly a fascinating foe, but making a minifigure costume based on such a spiny sea creature proved to be a design challenge. For this new, spiked mould, the process moved from concept sketches (1), to clay sculpting (2) and finally, plastic model (3) with printed torso and leg designs (4).

1   2   3   4

INVASION FORCE

The Shark Army is always ready to enforce the will of Garmadon – unless it gets too hard or too complicated. Some army members have battle experience, but many are just newly recruited amateurs. Garmadon's repeated failed attempts to take over Ninjago City mean that he's constantly having to refill his ranks.

Sharks ahoy • *Graphic art, Felicity Coonan* • The Shark Army's symbol speaks for itself and contains the name of their boss: "Garmadon".

Stick it, chop it or chain it to them! • LEGO *model development, Christopher Stamp* • The Shark Army fights with more than just bare fins: there's a whole arsenal of oceanic tools and weapons that come into play, incorporating fishy LEGO pieces in brand-new ways.

Marching to their master's beat • *Concept art, Kim Taylor* • The Shark Army falls in line under the command of their fearless yet winless leader, Garmadon.

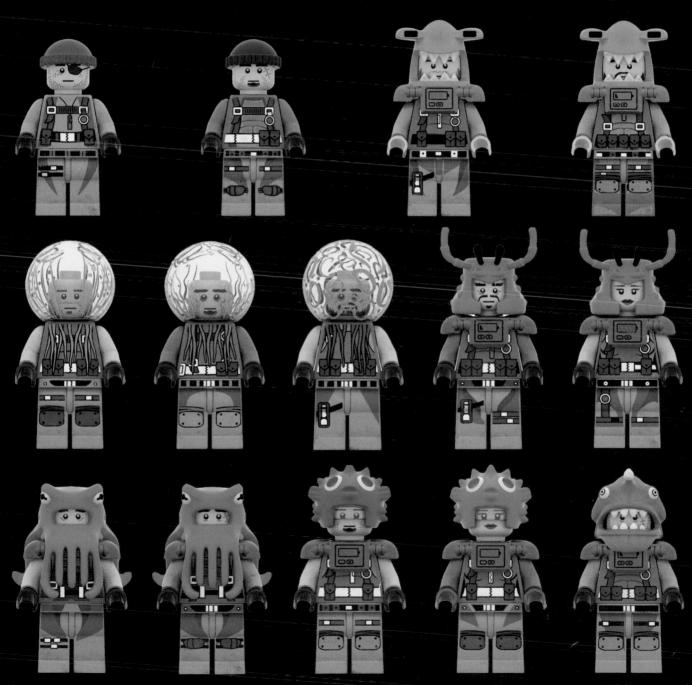

Minifigure militia • LEGO *model development, Djordje Djordjevic, Lars Roersen Nielsen, Marie Sertillanges* •
The Shark Army is a whole aquarium of sea-themed soldiers, with variants for many of the characters.

LORD GARMADON'S GENERAL #1

One would think that the title General #1 would come with prestige and respect, yet with Lord Garmadon it comes instead with the constant fear of being promptly replaced. It seems that General #1 only ever holds that position for a short time. Whenever Lord Garmadon is defeated by the ninja, he blows his top – and then swiftly blows his top general out of the volcano that marks his island headquarters.

Short-term shark
• *Concept art, Fiona Darwin* • This general is named #1 for only a brief period of time in the feature film. His fate sets the tone for what others might face after subsequent Garmadon battle losses.

Here comes General #2 • *Concept art, Fiona Darwin* • It's the turn of a female fighter to step up to the position of lead general. This lady lionfish-like minifigure had to swim through various schools of design thought before she found herself in her feature form.

Finalizing fins • *Concept art, Tim Pyman, Fiona Darwin* • These images show the designers honing in on the final concept for the female general. Robe, fin cape and hair all flow together for appeal and acceptable combat construct.

You're up, #2 • *Storyboard art, Natalie Wetzig* • In this scene, General #2 turned #1 has a hard time enjoying her party beverage while dealing with not-so-pleasant Lord Garmadon.

Fin fatale • *Concept work, Fiona Darwin; textile development, Nina Buch Rasmussen* • After sketching out flexible fin accessories for this general, the designer cut out paper versions of her cape and collar costume ideas to see what would work best. The LEGO Group then made a prototype with thin plastic.

So chilled • *Concept art, Fiona Darwin* • This general never loses her cool – as long as she has a refreshing beverage in hand. These are some of the many colourful concoctions she could have ordered from the LEGO drinks bar.

LOST GENERALS

Before there was a Shark Army, there was
a more varied array of costumed characters
who worked for Lord Garmadon and served
as his top generals. They, too, were
dishonourably discharged via volcanic
launch, leaving them singed and seething.

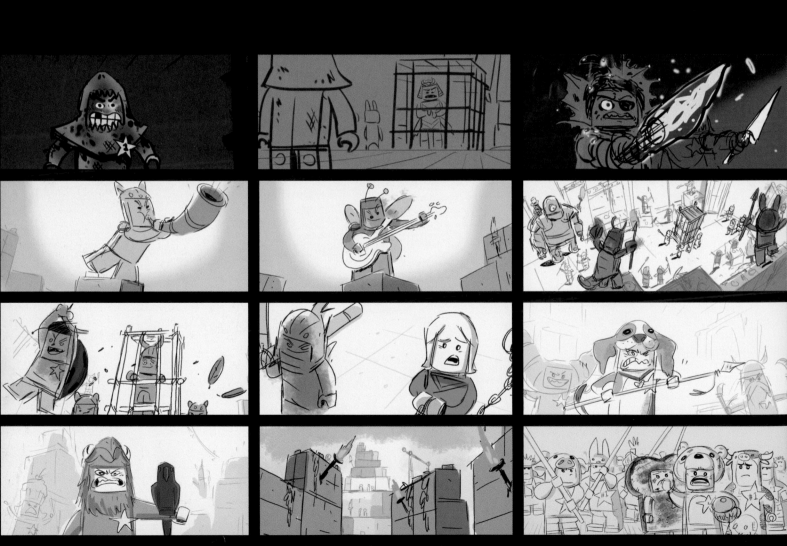

Showdown with the shot-outs • *Storyboard art, Januel Mercado and John Puglisi* • When Garmadon
finds himself face to face with the singed faces of his many former General #1s at their jungle lair,
things really heat up.

Angry and awkward • *Concept art, Fiona Darwin* • These preliminary minifigure designs were all considered as options for the gang of former generals living in the jungle and hoping to get their revenge on Garmadon.

Scorned and scorched • *Concept art, Marie Sertillanges (far left), Fiona Darwin; element development, the LEGO Group* • Ever wonder what the generals, and their starry badges, look like once they are fired out of the volcano? This line-up provides an up-close answer to that burning question.

IT GUYS

Beyond the brawn of the Shark Army, Lord
Garmadon also depends on the combined
brains of his IT crew. Their technological
talents help Garmadon to try and try again
to conquer Ninjago City and defeat the
pesky Secret Ninja Force.

All glassed up and ready to go · *Concept art, Kim Taylor* · This gaggle of goggle-eyed
IT engineers put their heads together to figure out the next best weapon for Garmadon
to try in his continual attempts to take over Ninjago City.

Show and tell · *Story panels, Ryan Savas* · The IT nerds meekly introduce
their latest invention to Garmadon, but this machine has nothing meek about it.

> **"B■ttle-cap glasses, themed t-shirts, somewhat questionable gr■■■ming, and excessive pr■te■tive wear all playe■ its part, but in the en■ the result was a fun ran■e of characters."**
>
> **Fiona Darwin, Concept Artist**

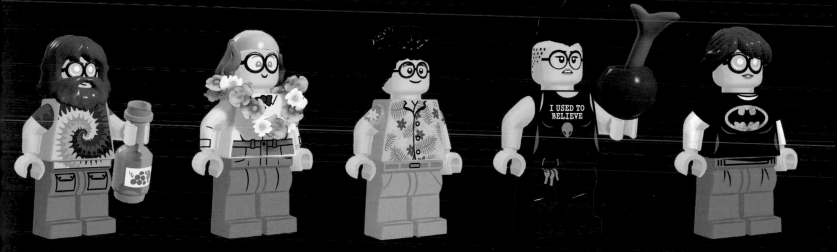

Oddly brilliant • *Concept art, Fiona Darwin* • When the IT team whip off their labcoats and get ready to party, their unique personalities shine.

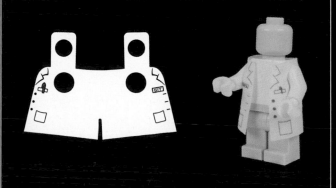

Cut-out coats • *Concept art, Fiona Darwin* • A most scientific way to approach the design of the labcoat, one of the early stages was to craft it out of paper first to see how it fitted on a minifigure. The result then moved to fabric development.

Ready, arm, fire • *Graphic art, Gibson Radsavanh* • The IT guys are equipped with plenty of computer gadgetry to do their mech-building for Garmadon. These decals show the many messages they may see on a daily, shark-firing, basis.

Hustle and bustle • *Concept art, Kim Taylor* • A rooftop marketplace is alive with the energy and activity of the happy citizens of Ninjago City. There's even a panda and a trumpeter amongst the crowds.

NINJAGO CITY CITIZENS

From sumo wrester to sushi chef, flower seller to taco guy, the citizens of Ninjago City are a mixed bag of minifigure fun. No matter how diverse they are, they all get along just fine – so why can't Lord Garmadon accept that fact and leave them in peace?

Chaos ensues • *Final renders* • Lord Garmadon's arrival (yet again) strikes fear in each and every citizen of Ninjago City. He stops people in their tracks and brings traffic to a standstill.

Every walk of life • *Concept art, Fiona Darwin Nadia Attlee, Dudley Birch; LEGO minifigures (below), Djordje Djordjevic* • Ninjago City features a wide variety of citizens, some of which appear in physical Collectible Minifigure form (below).

Unikitty Popgirl

Sushi Chef

Guitar Rocker

MEOWTHRA

The effect of using the Ultimate Weapon is the summoning of destructive beast Meowthra. Meowthra was a virtual replication of a live cat, and matching the feline actor required an entire team of digital artists in order to simulate fur, skin and shading. Working Meowthra into scenes where animated LEGO bricks were crashing to the ground added a whole other level of technical challenge to the animation task at hand. In the end, the team crafted cute and believable action.

Cat Kong • *Concept art, Gibson Radsavanh* • The name Meowthra is actually a play on the 1960s monster movie *Mothra*, starring a colossal moth. Meowthra has approximately nine million hairs in order to make its scenes look realistic.

"Any scene with Meowthra is challenging. Everyone involved wanted to make sure that no cats were harmed in the making of this film."

Bob Logan, Director

CHARACTER DESIGNS THAT NEVER WERE

Part of the creative cinematic process is travelling down story paths that ultimately detour from the final film... but what fun characters you can meet along the way! Here is a look at a few that might have appeared in the movie if it had continued down an alternative story route.

Alternative army • *Concept art, Peter Commins, Mark Sexton, Fiona Darwin, Kim Taylor, Gibson Radsavanh* • *These snake-like characters could have served in Garmadon's army, considering the fact that the ninja have actually fought similar serpentine creatures in the past.*

A bounty of bounty hunters • *Concept art, Kim Taylor, Bob Logan, Gibson Radsavanh* • These various minifigures would have been sent on a hunting party in an earlier version of the story.

"THE BUTTERFLY MEN OF YORN"

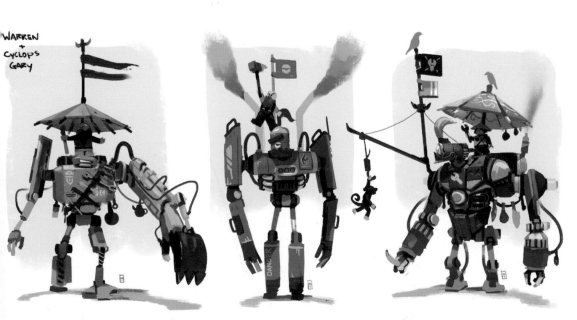

WARREN + CYCLOPS GARY

Warren and Cyclops Gary • *Concept art, Matt Betteker* • In one version of the story, the ninja meet one little and one much larger bounty hunter deep in the jungle. Named Warren and Cyclops Gary, their father and son relationship was designed to contrast strongly with Lloyd and Garmadon. Early concept art was wild and colourful.

One-eye on the prize
• LEGO *boost model, Luis F. E. Castaneda* • Brick-built options for Gary were trialled in a "boost" session, showing off his one eye and bold red colouring. His partner in crime is represented by a pre-exisiting LEGO minifigure.

VEHICLES

LLOYD'S DRAGON MECH

The Green Ninja often enters battle on his Dragon Mech (a term which is short for a mechanized suit or vehicle, like a wearable robot). Different concepts of what a dragon mech might look like preceded the organic-appearing – but brick-built – final version.

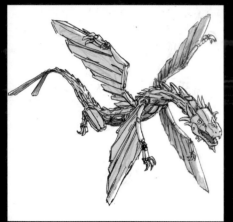

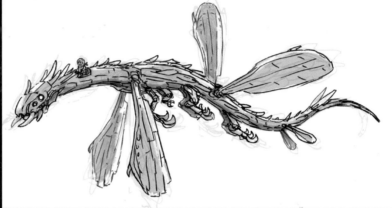

Dragon Sketches

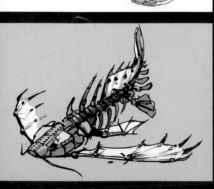

Winged wonder • *Concept art, Kim Taylor, Charles Santoso, Donald Walker* • Designers imagined many different winged dragons when creating the mech.

Help is here • *Concept art, Donald Walker, Kim Taylor* • Residents of Ninjago City cheer at the sight of the Green Ninja and his Dragon Mech coming to save them once again. In one piece of concept art, all of the ninja ride Dragon Mechs into battle.

> "Lloyd's Dragon Mech is a thing of beauty – it's whimsical and elegant, but also looks like it could be really effective in battle. It's an amazing design."

Paul Fisher, Writer/Director

Asian aesthetic • *Concept art, Adam Ryan* • The Green Dragon Mech was nearly, in fact, red, and is inspired by traditional Chinese New Year dragons.

A head above the rest · LEGO *boost models, Nicolaas Vás* · The Dragon Mech's development worked through many looks. Ideas ranged from Chinese dragons to pre-existing LEGO® builds, and from feathered finishes to the final, scaly result. In the final model, both the tongue and jawbone move to show the dragon roaring.

> **"**One of the biggest challenges with Lloyd's dragon was the custom brick element for the head. The dragon in the movie is physically much bigger than the toy so we had to create bricks that felt the same at the two scales, but were actually quite different moulds.**"**
>
> **Kim Taylor, Production Designer**

Color coordinating · *Concept art, Gibson Radsavanh, Jessica Sommerville* · Designers trialled various palette options including "greenie", "white knight" and "platinum." The colour scheme used on Lloyd's final mech is nicknamed "Goldie Hawn."

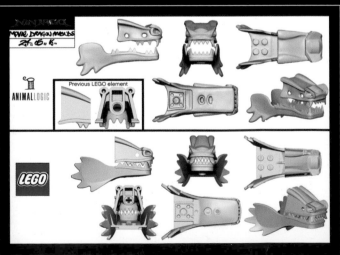

Heading up the design · *Design, Jessica Sommerville, Daniel Sri Sudarsono, Nicholas Timothy Whitmore* · In creating the Dragon Mech's head, designers applied different details to the facial features. After trying pre-existing bricks, new jaw and snout pieces were moulded.

Mini or maxi • LEGO *model development, Christopher Stamp (above), Michael Svane (right)* • Actual models of the Dragon Mech show it in both micro build and full-size scale. The flow of the design is evident in both builds, but which one would you rather face in battle?

Mean and green • *Final render* • The design team took great care in figuring out how the Green Ninja would be seated within his mech's cockpit. In full-on fighting mode, Lloyd and his Dragon Mech become one seamless fighting machine, complete with missiles firing from the mech's mouth.

Beauty rises above · *Final artwork, Dudley Birch* · The Green Ninja and his Dragon Mech take flight over the city in all their green, golden and glimmering glory.

NYA'S WATER STRIDER MECH

Playing on the Silver Ninja's elemental power of Water, this mech is as deft and light-footed as a pond skater insect. Its footpads make it versatile enough to walk on both land and water – perfect for keeping one step ahead of Lord Garmadon and his army.

All in proportion • *Concept art, Vaughan Ling, Simon Whiteley* • Great considerations were taken in figuring out the right dimensions for the legs, joints and footpads so as to avoid a misstep with this mech.

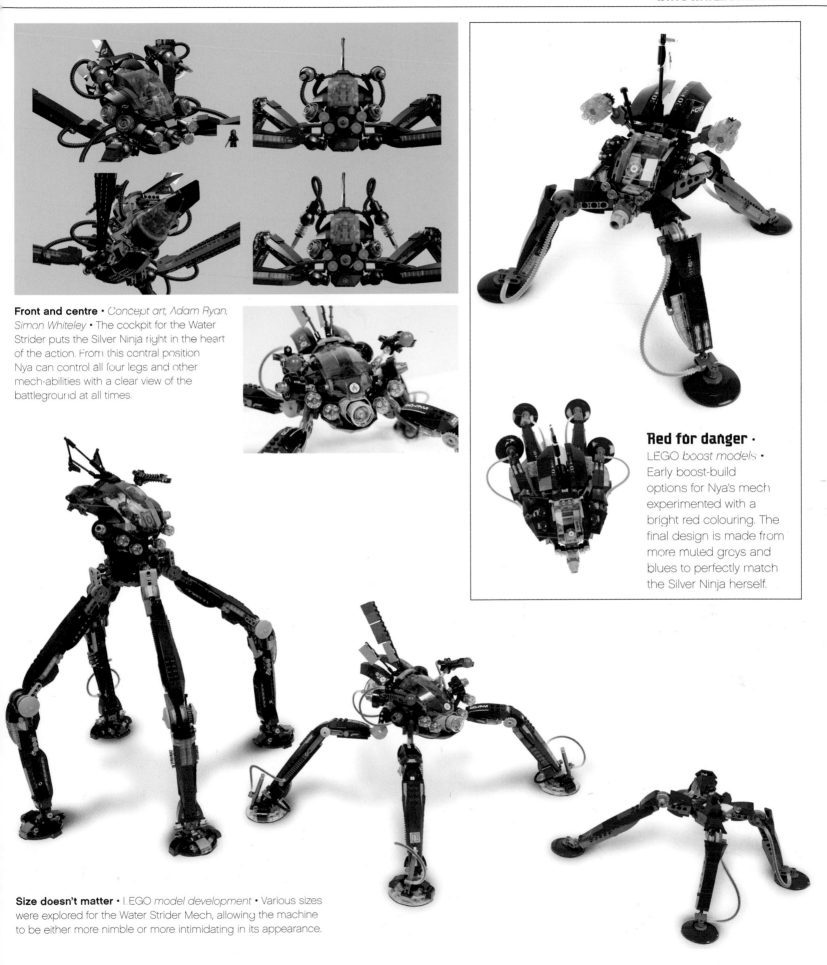

Front and centre • *Concept art, Adam Ryan, Simon Whiteley* • The cockpit for the Water Strider puts the Silver Ninja right in the heart of the action. From this central position Nya can control all four legs and other mech-abilities with a clear view of the battleground at all times.

Red for danger • LEGO *boost models* • Early boost-build options for Nya's mech experimented with a bright red colouring. The final design is made from more muted greys and blues to perfectly match the Silver Ninja herself.

Size doesn't matter • LEGO *model development* • Various sizes were explored for the Water Strider Mech, allowing the machine to be either more nimble or more intimidating in its appearance.

Walking on water and walls •
Concept art, Kim Taylor • With the dynamic footpads on this insect-like mech, the Silver Ninja can transport herself along all kinds of surfaces, at different angles. Nothing can slow down this mech – much to Lord Garmadon's dismay.

Leaping into action • *Final render •* The Water Strider Mech can spring out of the water faster than a flying fish, or a shark, which is useful considering the ninja's current foes.

Twice the fun • LEGO *model development, Li-Yu Lin (above), Nicolaas Vás (below)* • Both the micro and full-size final builds of the Water Strider Mech convey its delicate-looking but definitely ninja worthy construction.

"As we were designing the various mechs, I think I changed my mind about which one was my favourite every single day!

Simon Lucas, LEGO Senior Creative Director

COLE'S QUAKE MECH

Cole's elemental power is Earth, so it's fitting that his mech is synonymous with shaking the ground. Early ideas for the Quake Mech began with it digging into the ground with powerful tools, and later progressed to it vibrating with powerful sound effects.

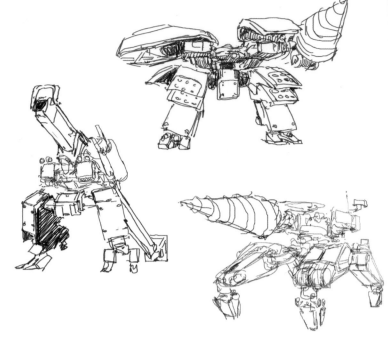

Compact design, cabin on drill

Drill hammer on arm, cabin on side

Multiple pivoting arms, cabin in centre

Drillin' and chillin' • *Concept art, Tim Pyman (above left), Vaughan Ling* • Rock-breaking strength was the main thrust of early mech designs for the Black Ninja's Quake Mech. Various forms of ground-bearing transportation, such as wheels, belts, or feet, were attached.

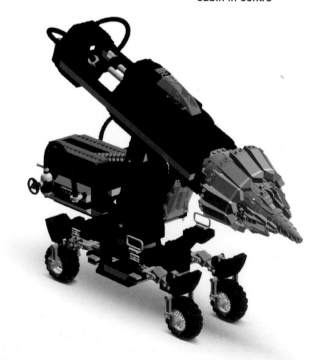

"Cole's single-wheeled mech with its big heavy bass speaker weapon is like nothing I have ever seen at the LEGO Group."

Simon Lucas, LEGO Senior Creative Director

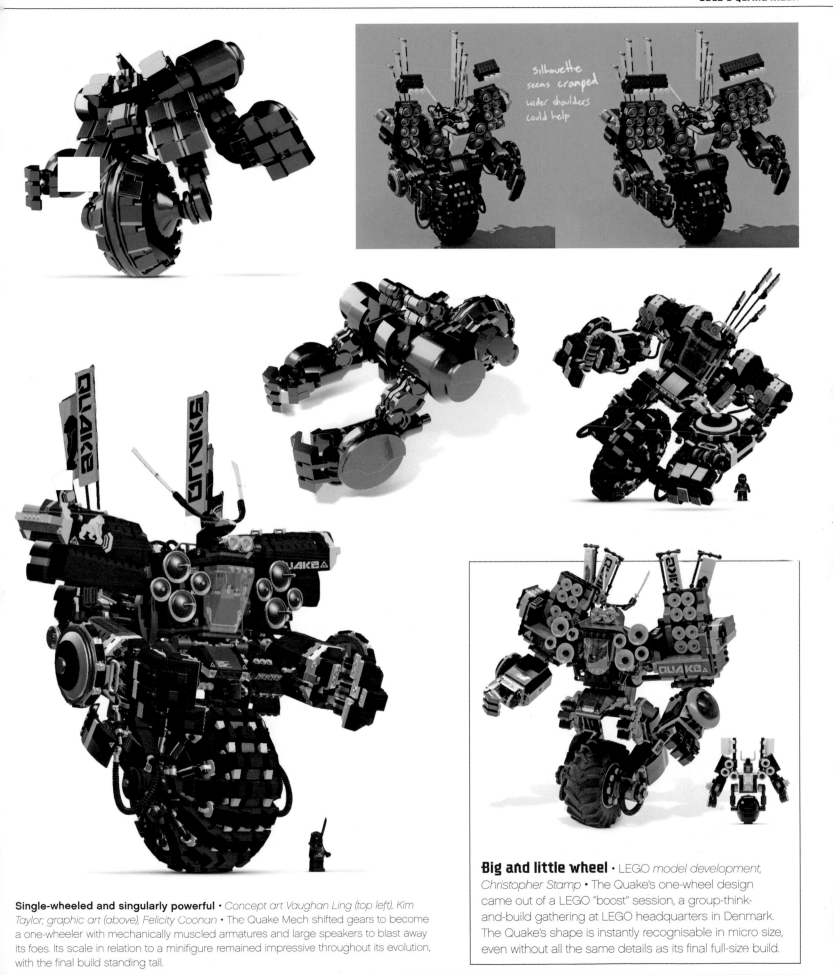

silhouette seems cramped wider shoulders could help

Single-wheeled and singularly powerful • *Concept art Vaughan Ling (top left), Kim Taylor; graphic art (above), Felicity Coonan* • The Quake Mech shifted gears to become a one-wheeler with mechanically muscled armatures and large speakers to blast away its foes. Its scale in relation to a minifigure remained impressive throughout its evolution, with the final build standing tall.

Big and little wheel • *LEGO model development, Christopher Stamp* • The Quake's one-wheel design came out of a LEGO "boost" session, a group-think-and-build gathering at LEGO headquarters in Denmark. The Quake's shape is instantly recognisable in micro size, even without all the same details as its final full-size build.

Loud and proud · *Concept art, Yannick Tan* · The Quake asserts its
strength through its earth-kicking wheel and its ground-shaking
sound system, making it a seismic powerhouse for the ninja.

Blasting sound and breaking glass · *Final render (top); LEGO model development (above); graphic art (right), Fiona Darwin* · From his seat in the cockpit of the Quake Mech, Cole can reach behind his steering module and grab whichever vinyl record will reverberate the right beat to shatter his opponent. The loud, pounding beats may even shatter his own windshield!

KAI'S FIRE MECH

The Red Ninja uses the elemental power of Fire, and his mech certainly rises (often in temperature) to the occasion as well as its ninja driver. Kai and his armed, flame-firing Fire Mech are often first on the scene.

Engine ingenuity • *Concept art, Vaughan Ling, Tim Pyman* • Early renditions of the Fire Mech show designers channelling traditional fire-engine aesthetics. This worked well when the concept was shooting water to put out fires, but the mech soon developed into becoming a fire launcher itself. Far more Red Ninja!

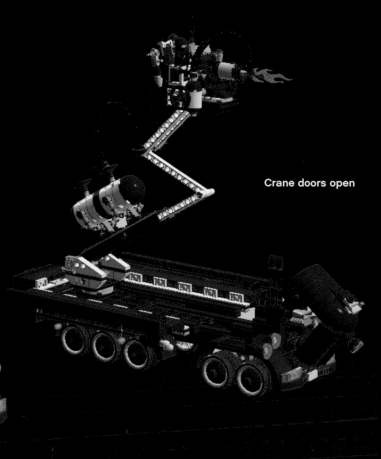

Crane doors open

Crane doors closed

Tanks for the help • *Concept art, Vaughan Ling* • An earlier biped mech design had water tanks on its back. This way the Red Ninja could potentially put out fires rather than torching things himself.

Big, bold, and boosted • *LEGO model development, Nicolaas Vás (bottom left), Mark Stafford (bottom middle and right)* • Brainstorming in a LEGO "boost session" for the Fire Mech resulted in a number of fascinating model builds, all quite impressive in scale with a minifigure.

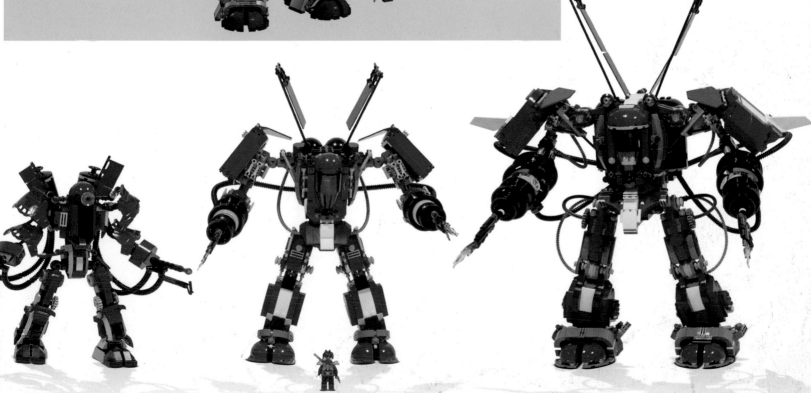

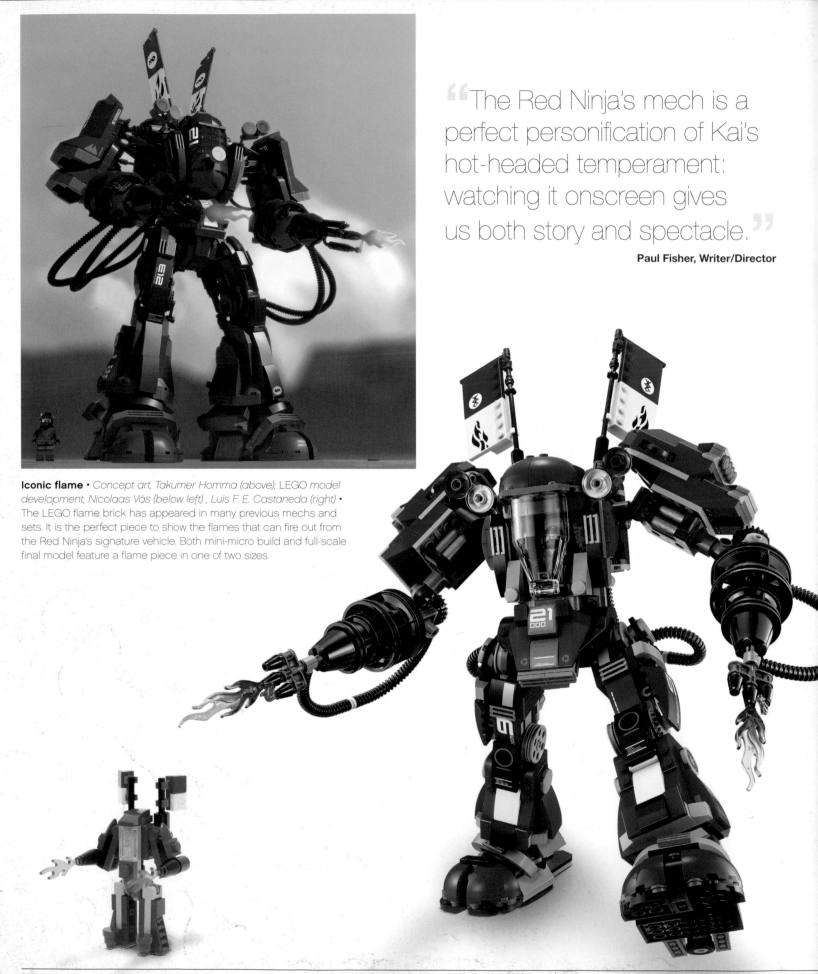

"The Red Ninja's mech is a perfect personification of Kai's hot-headed temperament: watching it onscreen gives us both story and spectacle."

Paul Fisher, Writer/Director

Iconic flame • *Concept art, Takumer Homma (above); LEGO model development, Nicolaas Vás (below left) , Luis F. E. Castaneda (right)* • The LEGO flame brick has appeared in many previous mechs and sets. It is the perfect piece to show the flames that can fire out from the Red Ninja's signature vehicle. Both mini-micro build and full-scale final model feature a flame piece in one of two sizes.

Larger than life · *Concept art, Kim Taylor* · As Kai's huge Fire Mech walks by on a mission to save Ninjago City, a bystander is left feeling very small. The mechs may be mighty and marvellous, but they also come hand-in-hand with battles and ensuing destruction.

Fire when ready · *Final render* · This hot-handed mech is prepared to flare up at a moment's notice.

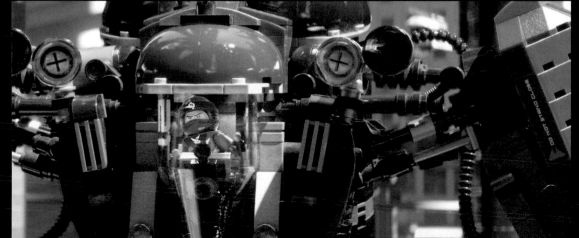

In the driver's seat · *Final render* · The Red Ninja drives his Fire Mech with great focus and hot-headed energy.

ZANE'S ICE TANK MECH

Channelling the element of Ice is what the White Ninja does during battle. His mech needs to keep up with his frozen focus in order to take down Lord Garmadon.

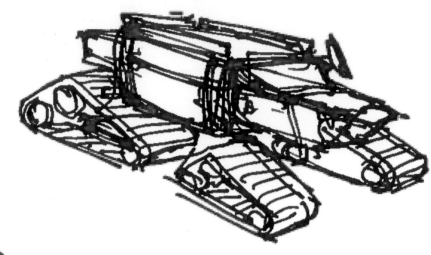

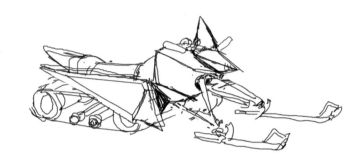

Elongated snowmobile with cabin weight to rear

Elongated snowmobile with skis at rear

Retro snowmobile with caterpillar tracks

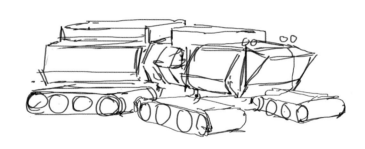

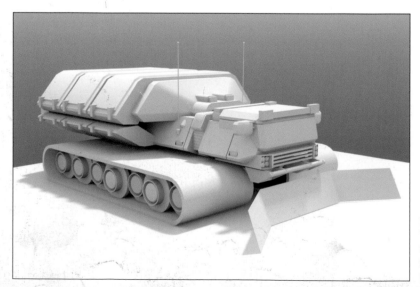

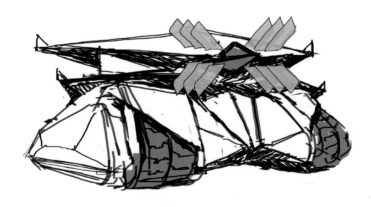

Frozen fighter • *Concept art, Tim Pyman (top left), Vaughan Ling (above and left)* • Designers looked to snowmobiles, snow ploughs, skis and snow cats for inspiration in developing the most chill mech for the White Ninja.

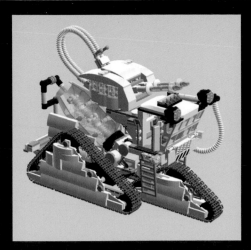

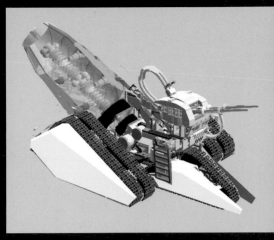

Belted on for action • *Concept art, Simon Whiteley, Adam Ryan, Vaughan Ling* • Caterpillar tracks quickly became a necessity for the Ice Tank. Hence bulldozer-like belts for transportation combine with a variety of weaponry.

ZANE Tank shooting function development

1 WIP Model: missing side cannon

2 Main doors open up

3 The cannon pivots forward

4 The door can close around the cannon

Now you see it... • LEGO *model development, Christopher Stamp (left), Nicolaas Vás (above)* • Early concept work showed the mech with sliding doors on top that could open out (1–2) to reveal a pivoting cannon that could rise up (3–4) to fire as needed.

Piloting patrol · *Final render (above);
concept art (left), Kim Taylor* · The White Ninja
surveys the battleground from his icy blue
cockpit. From its low-down position, Zane
remains close to the roadside action.

A chip off the old ice block · LEGO *model,
Li-Yu Lin (above right), Nicolaas Vás (left)* ·
Cool design planes and angles give both the
micro and maxi-builds of the Ice Tank Mech
a unique, glacier-like silhouette.

Frosty beverage maker and foe fighter all in one
• LEGO *model development* • The back of Zane's mech model comes complete with slushie-making machinery. With this, Zane can stay ice cool and hydrated at all times!

" I wanted to push the scale and make the vehicles feel like huge robots… I wanted them all to feel like they really worked, so we talked a lot about the internal mechanics as well as the overall shape. "

Charlie Bean, Director

Slushie to go • *Concept art, Kim Taylor* • As Zane's mech rolls into action, the rear slushie maker can be seen to be preparing a refreshing drink for Zane for when the fighting stops.

JAY'S LIGHTNING JET MECH

The Blue Ninja utilises the elemental power of Lightning in his fighting efforts. It was that characteristic that sparked the idea for his Lighting Jet Mech to be a shockingly cool, airborne vehicle.

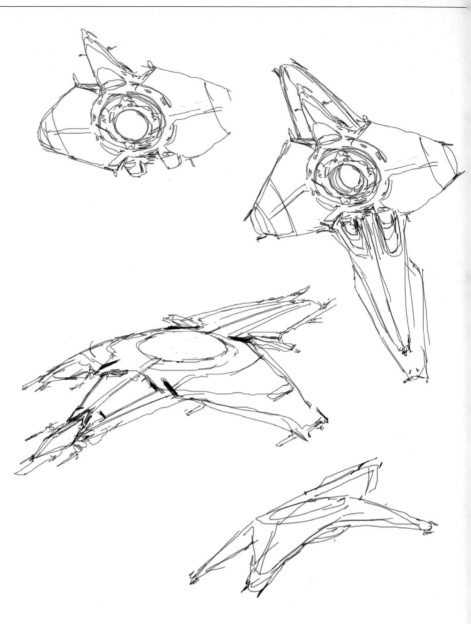

Self-generated power • *Concept art, Vaughan Ling (top right), Tim Pyman (above), Simon Whiteley (right)* • Early sketches of the Blue Ninja's mech echo the shape of an electrical generator in a more car-like style of vehicle. Many flying options were trialled: from aeroplane to flying-disc style vehicles. At one point Jay's mech was even called the Jaybird.

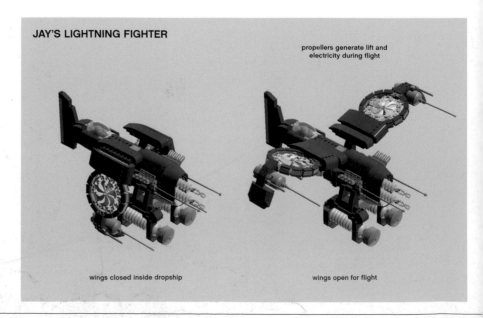

JAY'S LIGHTNING FIGHTER

propellers generate lift and electricity during flight

wings closed inside dropship

wings open for flight

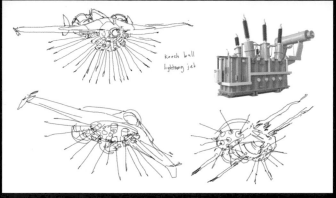

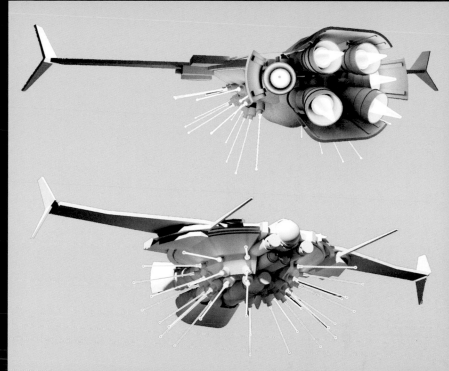

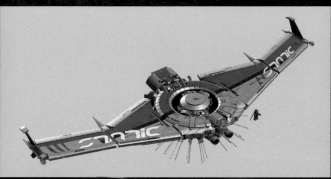

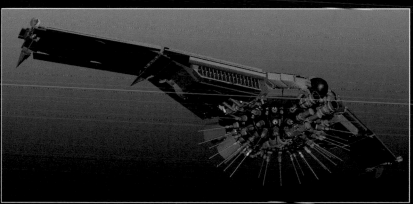

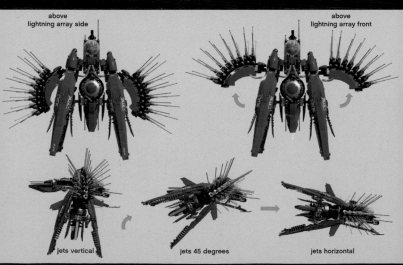

Spikey spacecraft · *Concept art, Vaughan Ling (top), Simon Whiteley and Adam Ryan (above)* · The Lightning Jet's evolution led to a design that involved many prongs. This version can also fold its wings underneath for a greater range of in-flight and landing capabilities.

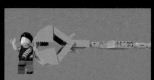

Gotcha! · *Concept art, Jessica Sommerville* · The mech design features a long "grabber" that might be used to pick up and save helpless Ninjago citizens who are mere moments away from impending doom.

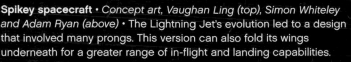

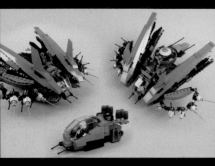

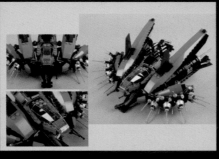

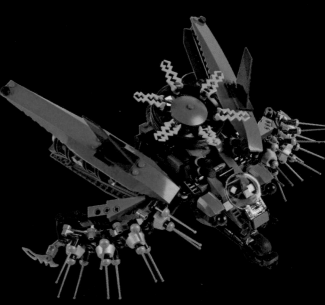

Blue-bird bird's eye view • *Concept art (top), Gibson Radsavanh; LEGO model development (above and right), Nicolaas Vás* • Each of the ninja's mechs are designed with a unique cockpit shape. A fighter-jet approach (middle) was considered for Jay before a helicopter-style cockpit (above left and right) was settled upon.

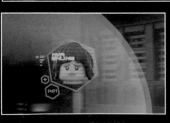

Strapped in and ready to fly • *Concept art (left), Felicity Coonan; storyboard art (above), Maggie Kang* • The cockpit area of Jay's mech is loaded with high-tech projection readouts and many other fun electrical details for the Blue Ninja to utilise in his battle efforts. From there he can communicate with his fellow ninja.

Lighting up the sky • *Concept art, Yannick Tan* • As this mech takes flight, it's more impressive than a thunderstorm when it flashes its lighting-blue bolts.

Making their point • *LEGO model, Nicolaas Vás (left), Aske Klejnstrup Garling (right)* • Whether in micro-build or full-size model format, the Lightning Jet Mech is a electrifyingly unique vehicle that stands as a prime example of how "the sky's the limit" when building with LEGO bricks.

GARMADON'S SHARK MECH

Lord Garmadon first fights alongside his Shark Army in his very own Shark Mech. This mech could have very well been a different dangerous sea creature, according to the designs that swam out of the creative development process.

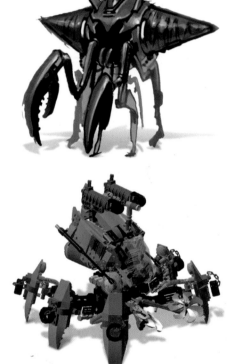

Creepy crawlers • *Concept art, Peter Commins, Gibson Radsavanh; LEGO development, Aaron Anderson* • Early versions of this mech were crab-like, with pincers and hard-shelled backs.

Is it a shark or a dog? • *Concept art, Vaughan Ling, Gibson Radsavanh, Kim Taylor* • These versions explored the possibilities of adding canine-like front and back legs to a shark, and even multiple heads. This design came to be known as a "Cerbershark" creature, referring to the three-headed dog, Cerbeus, from Greek mythology.

Parked shark • *Concept art, Simon Whiteley* • Annotated notes explain the multifunctional possibilites of this shark mech.

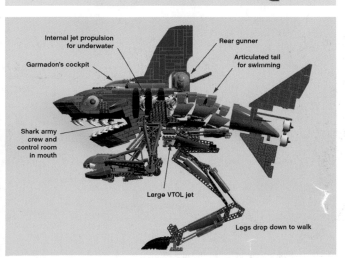

Internal jet propulsion for underwater

Rear gunner

Garmadon's cockpit

Articulated tail for swimming

Shark army crew and control room in mouth

Large VTOL jet

Legs drop down to walk

By land or by sea? • LEGO *model development, Luis F. E. Castaneda* • A shark that has legs, a cannon, and a claw – what more could an evil warlord want in a mode of transportation and destruction? A LEGO "boost session" took all these elements into account and brainstormed an impressive finished model for Lord Garmadon.

GARMA MECHA MAN

When Garmadon's IT guys come up with a new and improved mech for him, it's certainly bigger, badder and better – and it even fires out live sharks! This upright, samurai-style Mecha Man also emits a fiery glow that gives Garmadon an even more imposing presence, as if this huge machine were not fearsome enough.

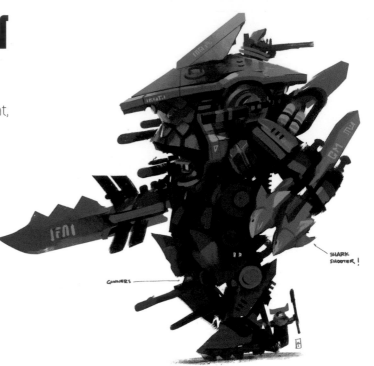

SHARK SHOOTER!

GUNNERS

A formidable foe • *Concept art, Gibson Radsavanh (above), Matt Betteker (top right)* • The Garma Mecha Man is the ultimate samurai warrior. The machine may have featured a wide variety of weapons, according to these early designs.

> "Hands down, Garmadon's Mecha Man is the best mech, because you can kick butt and get rock-hard glutes at the same time."
>
> **Bob Logan, Writer/Director**

Embroiled in battle • *Concept art, Matt Betteker* • It's Garmadon's Mecha Man vs the Green Ninja's Dragon Mech on the streets of Ninjago City – a big battle that's certain to leave a wave of destruction in its wake.

Mecha marching • *Concept art, Gibson Radsavanh* • As Lord Garmadon marches through the smoking battlefield, the tank on the mech's back can be seen to still be brimful of sharks.

Sharky and scary • LEGO *model development* • As the mech design progressed, it continued to combine the fearsome samurai look from early sketches, with shark-inspired details to complement Garmadon's Shark Army.

Command central • *Storyboard art (top), Januel Mercado; concept art, Gibson Radsavanh* • The cockpit right inside the mech mouth offers Garmadon power close to his multi-armed grasp, but apparently not enough cupholders or space for snacks.

Say what? • *Graphic art, Noemie Cauvin* • In case you can't read Ninjago Language, the torpedoes read "bye bye", making Lord Garmadon's intentions and attitude clear.

Mega mech • LEGO *model development, Luis F. E. Castaneda* • Due to LEGO scale requirements, the final model launches LEGO fish instead of sharks.

Ablaze with rage • *Concept art, Yannick Tan* • Lord Garmadon feels at home in his volcanic lair. He thus seeks to bring a similar fire with him wherever he and his Mecha Man roam in their efforts to take over Ninjago City.

SHARK ARMY VEHICLES

With an entire ocean's worth of inspiration, the designers made quite a splash in their exploration of vehicles for the Shark Army. Combining the most unique works of Mother Nature with fun LEGO technology, this creative effort was swimmingly successful.

Crustaceans, mollusks, and squid, oh my! • *Concept art, Peter Commins* • Sea creatures that might translate into vehicles rose from a deep well of creativity, including a "Great White Microsub" (above) and a "Skuttletank" (below left).

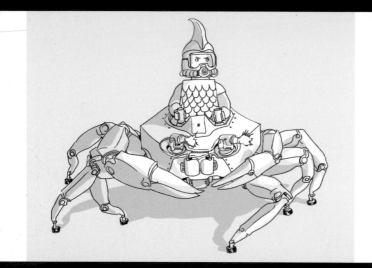

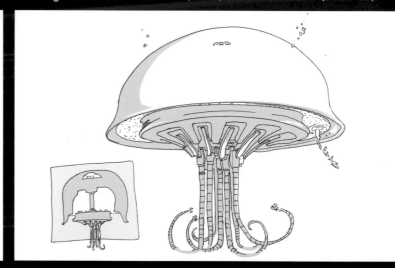

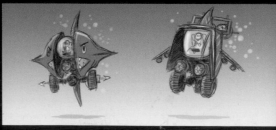

An army with a bite, or a pinch • *Concept art, Adam Murphy* • Lights, wheels, cockpits and weaponised pincer arms all feature amongst these early concept sketches, where Garmadon's army advances along the sea floor.

Naturally inspired ingenuity • *Concept art, Peter Commins* •
Whether using an anglerfish or a fiddler crab for inspiration,
designers show how these vehicles could work to Garmadon's
benefit – with mouths for swallowing intruders whole!

Under the sea • *LEGO boost images* •
Boost sessions of model building and
brainstorming at LEGO headquarters
resulted in a mechanically masterful
menagerie of vehicular creatures.

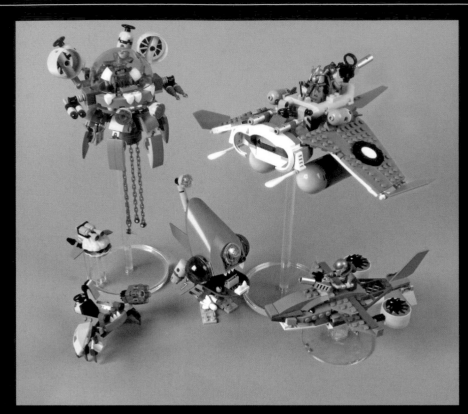

Shark-infested skies · LEGO *model development, Christopher Stamp, Jonas Norlen, Nicolaas Vás* · During model-building sessions, several Shark Army vehicle designs rose quickly to the surface as forerunners for further development work. A manta ray, a jelly sub and a crab mech were selected for working into physical LEGO models ahead of options that also included sharks, clams and piranhas.

Sharks

Piranhas

Clams

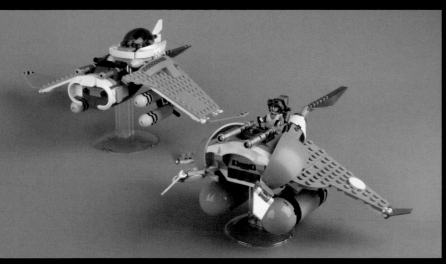

MANTA RAY

• LEGO *model development, Leonardo Francisco Lopez, Christopher Stamp* • The Manta Ray Mech is one of the vehicles featured in the army fleet. This craft is a fin-tastic addition to Garmadon's forces.

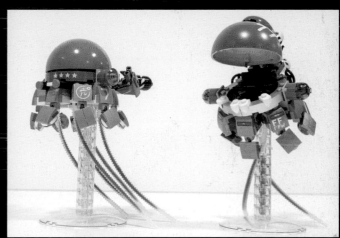

JELLY SUB

• LEGO *model development, Jonas Norlen, Christopher Stamp* • The Jellyfish mech can plumb the depths of the sea so that Garmadon doesn't miss a beat (or a barnacle).

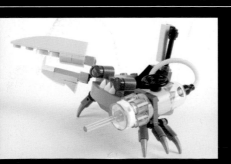

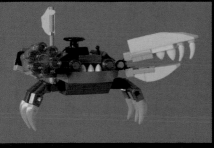

CRAB MECH

• LEGO *model development, Li-Yu Lin, Christopher Stamp* • The Shark Army's underwater fleet can scuttle around the battlegrounds in this hard-shelled vehicle.

NINJAGO CITY VEHICLES

The hustle and bustle of Ninjago City means its citizens have a lot of things to do, places to go... and so they need a variety of ways to get there! In true LEGO form, the vehicles they use are a perfect balance of fun and function.

Red seaplane

Lucky Duck **seaplane**

By air • LEGO *model development* • When the skies are not filled with mech battles, the citizens can convey themselves via planes such as these.

Movement in the market place • LEGO *model development* • A LEGO "boost session" of brainstorming with bricks brought about this fun set-up that includes vehicles such as carts and scooters... and a good, old-fashioned cow as well.

The *Crystal White* **large junk cargo**

Solar-powered skiff

Beer skiff

Lucky junk

The *Sea Monkey*

Kimsee tour boat

By sea • LEGO *model development* • With Ninjago City being a waterfront community, the designers let many boat designs float out of their creativity and into physical brick form.

By land • LEGO *model, Dimitrios Stamatis (bottom right); graphic art, Felicity Coonan* • A wide variety of vehicles are needed in a town as active as Ninjago City. Think of just how fast the citizens can get around in that speedy monorail train!

Grinder bike

Ox-drawn tea and sake cart

Taxi tuk

Ambulance tuk

Pretzel cart

Ice-cream van

Chicken man tuk

Monorail train

Police tuk

Streetsweeper

City waste truck

On the road • *Concept art, Grant Freckelton* • It's a wonder everyone can get to where they need to be without any traffic lights in sight... but as with everything brick-built, it all comes together perfectly!

**Producer Dan Lin (right) and
Head of Story Maggie Kang (left)**
Photography (right) by Steve Cohn

AUTHOR ACKNOWLEDGEMENTS

I am honoured to have been invited behind the scenes once again to tell the story of
the LEGO Group/Warner Bros./Animal Logic collaborative cinematic process. I appreciate
the filmmaking crew that somehow found time to share their knowledge and experience
with me while crafting this ambitious movie, with extra gratitude going out to Toby Gibson
who valiantly served as our "communications central" while working on the film.

I thoroughly enjoyed working with the organised, talented and thoughtful team at
DK Publishing, especially Emma Grange who was an amazingly close and supportive
partner, even with an entire continent and ocean between us.

I am ever grateful for my own team of family and friends who are an awesome force
in my life, even if they don't have secret ninja skills (as far as I know), and I thank them
for their continued love and support.

– TMZ

DK ACKNOWLEDGEMENTS

DK would like to thank the many artists around the world
who have helped to make this book possible, and those who have provided information,
answered interview questions, and generally provided ninja-like assistance across
multiple time zones. Special thanks go to Kim Taylor, Felicity Coonan and Toby Gibson at
Animal Logic, and Simon Lucas and the LEGO NINJAGO team in Billund.

Thanks also to Ben Harper, Melanie Swartz, Melissa Jolley, Melissa Crow
and Nick Gligor at Warner Bros., Randi Sørensen, Heidi K Jensen, Paul Hansford
and Martin Leighton Lindhart at the LEGO Group, everyone at Animal Logic,
and Keith Malone and Nelson LaMonica.

At DK, thanks to Laura Palosuo and Rona Skene
for editorial help, and Nathan Martin and Jon Hall for design assistance.

Director Charlie Bean
*Photography by
Eric Charbonneau*

The Warner Bros. team
Photography by Garrett Cox

The Animal Logic team
Photography by Chris Swinbanks

CONTRIBUTING ARTISTS

Adam Murphy, Adam Ryan, Ben Walker, Bob Logan, Carey Yost, Charles Santoso, Charlie Bean, Chris Reccardi, David Whittaker, Donald Walker, Dudley Birch, Eric Ramsey, Felicity Coonan, Fiona Darwin, Gaelle Seguillon, Gibson Radsavanh, Grant Freckelton, Heiko Drengenberg, Januel Mercado, Jessica Sommerville, Joe Feinsilver, John Puglisi, Kim Taylor, Kristen Anderson, Lianne Hughes, Maggie Kang, Marie Sertillanges, Mark Sexton, Michael Halford, Nadia Attlee, Natalie Wetzig, Noemie Cauvin, Paul Fisher, Paul M. Wood, Peter Commins, Pierre Salazar, Ryan Savas, Simon Whiteley, Takumer Homma, Tim Pyman, Vaughan Ling, Yannick Tan

CONTRIBUTING FILM CAST AND CREW

Jackie Chan, Dave Franco, Justin Theroux, Alex Fry, Alexis Jacobson, Bob Logan, Bradley Sick, Charlie Bean, Craig Welsh, Dan Lin, Dudley Birch, Fabian Müller, Felicity Coonan, Fiona Chilton, Fiona Darwin, Greg Jowle, Ingrid Johnston, Josh Murtack, JP Le Blanc, Julie Rogers, Kim Taylor, Kristen Murtha, Maggie Kang, Maryann Garger, Matt Everitt, Miles Green, Paul Fisher, Simon Lucas

AT THE LEGO GROUP

Simon Lucas, Brian Nielsen, Leonardo Francisco Lopez, Nicolaas Johan Bernardo Vás, Luis F. E. Castaneda, Li-Yu Lin, Michael Svane Knap, Christopher Leslie Stamp, Aske Klejnstrup Garling, Dimitrios Stamatis, Mark John Stafford, Karl Oskar Jonas Norlen, Carl Thomas Merriam, Matt Betteker, Stewart Whitehead, Niels Milan Pedersen, Nicholas Timothy Whitmore, Paul Marion Wood, Esa Petteri Nousiainen, Carsten Lind, Jakob Rune Nielsen, Djordje Djordjevic, Lars Roersen Nielsen, Marie Sertillanges, Mark Tranter, Desiree Muller, Tara Wike, Nina Buch Rasmussen, Aaron Anderson, Niek Duco van Slagmaat, Daniel Sri Sudarsono

ADDITIONAL ARTWORK
Cover art Kim Taylor
Additional artwork page 3: Tim Pyman; page 6–7: Ben Walker; page 28–29: Gibson Radsavanh; page 94–95: Ben Walker; page 198-199: Gibson Radsavanh; endpapers: Peter Commins.

The LEGO team
Photography by Tim Troejborg

Senior Editor Emma Grange
Senior Designer Lisa Robb
Editors Beth Davies and Rosie Peet
Designers Sam Bartlett, Jenny Edwards,
Toby Truphet and Rhys Thomas
Creative Technical Support Tom Morse and Andy Bishop
Pre-production Producer Siu Chan
Producer Louise Daly
Managing Editor Paula Regan
Design Manager Jo Connor
Publisher Julie Ferris
Art Director Lisa Lanzarini
Publishing Director Simon Beecroft

Cover designed by Rhys Thomas

First published in Great Britain in 2017 by
Dorling Kindersley Limited
80 Strand, London WC2R 0RL
A Penguin Random House Company

Page design copyright © 2017 Dorling Kindersley Limited
DK, a Division of Penguin Random House LLC

16 17 18 19 10 9 8 7 6 5 4 3 2 1
001–299079–Sep/2017

Printed and bound in China

A WORLD OF IDEAS:
SEE ALL THERE IS TO KNOW

www.dk.com
www.LEGO.com

Master Wu's Secret Ninja Force
• *Concept art, Fiona Darwin* •